I DARE YOU TO
GROW

What people are saying about I DARE YOU TO GROW

When I heard Pastor Yesenia Then preach the first time, I understood that I was before a woman who represents the new generation of preachers that our times demand. Her ministry is sustained by a word of revelation and accompanied by a powerful anointing. Undoubtedly, this is what the church needs to advance in the promotion of Kingdom values.

Yesenia has her own unique style to communicate the Word of God. She is a woman with a profound revelation of the Scripture. As her friend and fellow minister, I understand that she has a special assignment from God for this time. I am convinced that this book will impact your life. When I read it, it was as if I was hearing her from a pulpit, with the grace and energy that she emanates.

This book will impact and bless you and as its title says, it will challenge you to grow where you have been planted. It will help you to break off all the limitations that inhibit you from moving forward to achieve your dreams and goals. And through it, you will learn to live according to God's purpose for your life.

—**Pastor Ruth Ureña**
Iglesia de Dios Príncipe de Paz, Fort Pierce, FL.

I DARE YOU TO GROW is a majestic work in which the author Yesenia Then puts in your hands a valuable resource for the achievement of your purposes in the Lord's vineyard.

If you have tried different strategies and you are interested in achieving your goals, this compelling work will open a new horizon to rid yourself from the statistics of the unsuccessful.

A careful reading of this written production will help you understand that to reach a reliable and sustained growth track, it is necessary to possess a full conviction and assurance of God's purpose in your life. You will understand that for the believer in Christ there are no rules or methods that can govern growth, if there's no obedience to the virtuous principles of God's Word. With great skill, the author illustrates that as we grow, our actions improve, and our spiritual stature rises remarkably.

One of the basic proposals of this book is an analytical study of the Holy Scriptures as the indispensable mean for spiritual growth.

Yesenia Then's challenge is very significant because it implies growing in every area of our life. It points to a goal that corresponds to what the apostle Paul said in Ephesians 4:13 "until we all reach unity in the faith and in the knowledge of the Son of God and become mature, attaining to the whole measure of the fullness of Christ."

Keep in mind that each challenge is an excellent opportunity to grow, take advantage of it; don't remain in inertia. Make use of the tools contained in this treasure of spiritual nature and experience the levels of glory to which you were appointed.

—**Lic. Mauro A. Vargas, M.Div**.
Chancellor, Iglesia de Dios Bible Seminary

The struggle with ourselves and our destiny is fought day to day, step by step, thoughts against thoughts. In this book, Yesenia Then helps the reader to renew the mind with updated, revealed, well-thought and compiled knowledge, profound and practical examples. She combines a perfect equation of teaching principles, concepts and insights that will result in the push that every believer needs to visualize a holy, victorious, productive, coherent, renewed, balanced life.

With a compelling insight, the substance of an edifying apostle and pastoral style, each chapter fulfills the objective of taking us to a peak that points to the next height. The natural attraction of reading this book promotes an appetite to overcome, to achieve excellence and a more significant weight of divine glory.

Yesenia hits the bull's eye when she eloquently describes the nature of the palm tree and its attributes, as a parallel of the righteous called to flourish and prosper, one of my favorite scriptures which I have preached in depth for a long time. I applaud this excellent content as well as its teachings regarding territories, order, spiritual warfare, Kingdom principles, unity and power, respect, authority and spiritual positions.

If we seek to grow in wisdom, renew our minds effectively and continue to uphold the cross with determination, which implies self-improvement and spiritual advancement, don't stop reading Yesenia's book, because your faith will connect with the knowledge that makes the difference!

— **Pastor Lucy Cosme**
Founder, Executive Director of the Villa Bendición Ministry

Growth is a natural, inevitable process. To grow, one must allot time, and in the end, we'll see that we've advanced. Here is the trick: grow unavoidably and wildly. The challenge presented by Pastor Yesenia is to grow in a productive and fruitful way. To achieve this, we must consider some conditions that people tend to overlook, even in things that pertain to Christian growth.

Some people are growing, but not in the proper sense, nor with the quality necessary to achieve a satisfactory result. That is what this book is about. The author explains with excellent clarity the fundamental aspects that must be considered to develop a spiritual and natural growth that glorifies the Lord and allows us to bear fruit to be a blessing to others. I invite you to read this vital contribution of Pastor Then, and together with her, I dare you to grow.

— Apostle Santiago Ponciano
Iglesia Tabernáculo de Adoración
Santo Domingo, Dominican Republic

I DARE YOU TO
GROW

In any terrain and at all levels

YESENIA THEN

DEDICATION

*T*o the Absolute Owner of my life, my King, Lord and Savior Jesus Christ, for having chosen me according to the pure affection of His will for the fulfillment of His purposes on Earth. Thank you, Lord, for the high honor you grant me by allowing me to serve you with my life. I love you, Jesus!

To my children, my two treasures José Miguel Liriano Jr. (Maiky) and Andy Isai Liriano, for their unconditional love, for understanding and being part of the ministry that God has entrusted to us.

ACKNOWLEDGMENTS

I want to especially thank Florentina Escaño, the woman that God used as a channel to bring me into the world, not only for being an excellent mother but also a great friend. Thank you, Mom, for your wise advice, for your unconditional support and for always keeping us in your prayers.

To the many men and women of God, who have inspired us; to my mentors, friends, colleagues in the ministry and to all those who have contributed in some way so that God's dream may flourish in us.

To my assistant Ana Karen Morillo and all the other members part of the International Ministry Soplo de Vida, for their dedication and selflessness in favor of the projects that the Lord has entrusted in our hands. Thank you, dear team, you are a blessing!

CONTENTS

FOREWORD

*I*n human existence, the most significant challenges are fought, and the fiercest and ruthless enemies face each other. It is a hostile struggle, in which an individual faces a task in an attempt for existence. It is the struggle between what I am, what I should be and what God designed me to be.

Often to approach these dilemmas of existence we do it through questions that point to the very essence of what we are. That is why we are not perplexed by the psalmist's question: What is man? Am I where I should be, or am I just here, not knowing why I am here, not knowing why I exist or who am I?

It's amid the diversity of questions and philosophical definitions, away from the essence and ultimate reason of a SUPREME BEING, that we come to the point where wisdom keeps quiet and philosophers fall silent. We loose the urge to ask and only yearn to know who we are; to know how I was known, to know the One who knew me, when not even one knows by oneself. For those God foreknew, declared the Apostle Paul, He foreknew who they are, where they would be and where He would take them to do what He only knew and understood, perhaps regardless of our limitations of concepts and existential voids.

All these questions are summarized by Abraham Maslow when presenting his known scale of human needs, defines self-realization as an essential need that marks the path for SELF-DISCOVERY, through a succession of experiences, in which you connect with your real self, and you live from that identity; and only if you feel that you are living an INTEGRAL, CREATIVE LIFE and you ENJOY IT, you feel that you are on the path to self-realization. It's worth mentioning that SELF-REALIZATION is the key to success.

Self-realization consists in developing our full potential to become everything we are. It is to become whole in fullness. The self-realization or realization of oneself has to do with authenticity, with being what one is, and not what one has learned or pretends to be, far from its truth or inner reality. "I want to be who I know I can be."

The problem of self-realization necessarily implies asking the existential questions Who am I? What am I?

The desire to grow is part of the human nature designed by God; the way in which we grow is the method, the process or the form. As you deepen into the intention of the author, she will defy you as she has dared me, to reach HIGHER LEVELS.

Yesenia Then, with the effusiveness of a Pentecostal preacher, charismatic and challenging, takes us through an extensive journey of the Scriptures from which she draws characters, for us to see how those that lived before us not only experienced life but also grew to higher levels. All this is an essential part of the Christian faith, the subjectivity of faith.

The approach of the textual imperatives of God's Holy Word is an essential part of the present book, where many passages of Scripture encourage us to move, to pass through, to grow.

Among the many riches of this book, I can point out that the viewpoint offered in the teaching of the fig tree as the property is compelling; the understanding of OWNERSHIP, where there is an OWNER that cares. The author says that someone plants into the dark but knows and expects fruit from the crop.

She also addresses the sense of belonging. I belong to a vineyard and the wine grower expects to harvest His fruit. What must I do? What must I remove to grow limitlessly to higher levels?

The author's wisdom, spirituality, and Christian maturity tell us: Don't fret about everything you lack, just increase your potential.

Other elements worthy of noticing and reflecting are the conjugations of the verbs, such as *multiply, improve, dig, fertilize, start* and *mark*. These verbs have an applicability that generates life and impulses us to grow.

I assure you that this book will not merely provoke you, it will also mark you, it will challenge you enormously, and it will help you to break down the walls that you never thought you could overcome.

I suggest not to read this book lightly but to internalize it and try to accept the opportunity to conquer the higher levels where God will take you.

Rev. Elvis Samuel Medina
Administrative Bishop, Iglesia de Dios
Dominican Republic

INTRODUCTION

$\mathcal{T}$he term growth denotes expansion, advancement, widening, and increase. That is why with just listening to it we are filled with optimism and inspiration for the realization. Everyone, no matter how little or how much we've achieved so far, can attain a higher level of growth. However, to reach it, it will be essential to have a clear and strong purpose of conquering it.

This book expresses the intention to challenge and give you some useful tools for you to achieve growth. Because as agents of the Lord, we represent His interests on Earth, and it is precisely with God's interest that you identify what He has designed you for and become everything He wanted you to be when He created you.

Your internal resources, such talents, gifts, and abilities, speak of the form the Lord wanted to give you. The place where you are today, (regardless of your present condition) represents the space where He wanted to put you. It would be impossible for you to have what you have and be where you are, if

God wouldn't have allowed it. On this basis, we can know that your Creator has expectations of you. God perfectly knows what you can attain, and He expects you to do it.

The desire to grow with which you are born that continues throughout the different stages of your life, is not accidental. It's the intention of God, placed in your heart so that you pursue the fulfillment of what He has already outlined for you.

For it is God who **works in you both to will and to do for His good pleasure** (Philippians 2:13-14).

For I know the plans I have for you," *declares the Lord, "plans to prosper you and not to harm you, plans to give you hope and a future* (Jeremiah 29:11 NIV).

So, let's make the Lord smile from the place where we are at, and continue to grow until we become everything that by His grace and His deposits, He expects us to be. Let's start the journey!

PART ONE

CALLED TO BEAR FRUIT

Chapter 1

THERE IS A COST

*Everything of value has a cost
and growth is no exception.*

THERE IS A COST

$\mathcal{Y}$our life will not be different, as long as your actions remain the same. Growth is not automatic, nor does it happen suddenly. The fact that you get up every day and dream of being better does not make you better.

If you genuinely want to become all that you are capable of being, you will need more than just desire; your intention should be so stubborn, to make you unstoppable against any obstacle. It is so strong, that your advancement does not depend on your state of mind and so marked, that you will not desist until the best version of you is revealed, the one God designed and placed within you before you were born.

For we are God's masterpiece. He has created us anew in Christ Jesus, so we can do the good things he planned for us long ago (Ephesians 2:10 NLT).

For you created my inmost being; you knit me together in my mother's womb. I praise you because I am fearfully and wonderfully made; your works are wonderful, I know that full well (Psalm 139:13-14 NIV).

However, even though your design was already drawn, and the deposits were made in you, the fact of making all that work depends on you.

For example, let's imagine that someone gives you the key to a robust 4x4 vehicle that has been specially designed to be driven on all terrain, including those that are rough and slippery, but if instead of driving it, you decide to keep it in the garage, its specialized design will do you no good. And if you only used it as a regular car on regular roads, the true capacity built into this "all terrain" vehicle would not be exposed.

In this sense, God has placed the key in your hand, but how you use it depends on you.

> *God has placed the key in your hand, but how you use it depends on you.*

What we are today is the result of what we decided to do yesterday; what we will be tomorrow depends greatly on what we do today.

Developing everything that was given to us and living according to our specialized design is determined by our daily actions.

One of the subtlest enemies of our progress is the continuous postponement that makes us live holding on to expressions like: "I will wait a while before starting, I will do it later, maybe I will get to it next year." And this, along with other hindrances is what stagnates us, leading us to live in "autopilot" mode.

So, what is the best time to start? The answer is: **Right now!** And the fact that you are reading this book confirms it.

What does growth imply?

In biological terms, growth implies a progression in the increase in body volume, which does not stop until it reaches its definitive shape and size. Growth is possible (among other processes), due to the assimilation of nutrients that enters our body, the byproduct of nutrition. Without adequate nutrition, growth will be deficient.

As in biological growth, growing in any other area also requires the proper nutrition. The area that demands the highest level of growth will vary from one person to another, but the principle (of adequate nutrition) will always be the same.

No one can grow for you; you are the one responsible for your progress.

Have you ever thought about taking what you are to its fullest expression? How could you align the deposits of talents, gifts, and abilities that were given to that version of you? What are you going to do to achieve it?

The reason why you seriously need to consider the answer to each one of these questions is simple: No one can grow for you. The only one responsible for your progress is you.

Others can motivate you and even inspire you but revealing your highest levels of growth will depend on you.

Make Headway

When it comes to growth, one of the most important aspects is to make headway. Stagnation, of which many people fall victim to is not always due to a lack of resources or opportunities but the lack of stability and discipline to achieve what they have planned. In a fiery way, they initiate more than one project, but they do not complete any of them; they enroll in the university, but they do not graduate. Almost everything they start is left unfinished, courses, the books they read and the assignments they are given. They have the motivation, but they lack steadfastness. They like the easy way; they prefer things that are quick, and their interests are focused on the events, not in the processes. This makes their lives unstable and lacking good results. As the Apostle James said:

> *Stagnation, of which many people fall victim to isn't always due to a lack of resources or opportunities but the lack of stability and discipline to achieve what they have planned.*

...*he is a double-minded man, **unstable in all his ways*** (James 1:8).

So, if the fact of being steadfast is so crucial to our growth, what should be done to achieve it?

I would recommend the following:

› *Seek the Lord's approval in what you do.*

If you want to have a genuine growth and become resistant to the different pressures that you will have to face as you move forward, you must count with God's approval in everything you do.

Many people carry out their plans and undertake projects that are based, not on the Lord's desire for them, but on emotions of the moment, on the recommendations they receive from others or the results they have seen in others doing the same. After having lost time and resources, they realize that their intentions, although not bad, were not based on the right fundamentals.

Aligning ourselves to God's plans for us should be the basis of everything we do.

Only then, will we have the absolute guarantee that we will do well.

> *Aligning ourselves to God's plans for us should be the basis of everything we do. Only then, will we have the absolute guarantee that we will do well.*

This is what the psalmist referred to when he said: *"Unless the Lord builds the house, they labor in vain who build it."* Based on this, we can deduce that **if the Lord builds the house, the destroyers labor in vain** (See Psalm 127:1).

So, if you know that you have God's approval in what you have begun, be steadfast; don't let yourself be dragged out by your emotions, close your ears to toxic comments that can divert you and don't look at things that can divert your focus.

› *Don't leave things half-way done*
More important than how you begin something is the way that you finish it. Even if you become weary

on the road, you don't feel the enthusiasm you felt at the beginning, don't give up and arm yourself with courage, because although it is not easy, I assure you that it will be much more difficult to consider in the end, what you would have acquired if you had not surrendered.

One of the most compelling biblical examples that we have about this is from the apostle Paul, who refers to the authenticity of his ministry when he said:

From the Jews five times I received forty stripes minus one. Three times I was beaten with rods; once I was stoned; three times I was shipwrecked; a night and a day I have been in the deep; in journeys often, in perils of waters, in perils of robbers, in perils of my own countrymen, in perils of the Gentiles, in perils in the city, in perils in the wilderness, in perils in the sea, in perils among false brethren; in weariness and toil, in sleeplessness often, in hunger and thirst, in fastings often, in cold and nakedness — besides the other things, what comes upon me daily: my deep concern for all the churches (2 Corinthians 11:24-28).

But in spite of everything, it is this same Paul who at the end of his apostleship, with all prosperity we hear him say:

I have fought the good fight, I have finished the race, I have kept the faith. Finally, there is laid up for me the crown of righteousness, *which the Lord, the righteous Judge, will give to me on that Day* (2 Timothy 4:7-8).

› *From the beginning, focus on the final reward*
Keeping in mind, from the beginning, what you will achieve in the end, will help you to maintain the focus.

On one occasion, while the renowned sculptor Michelangelo was chiseling a block of marble, one of his students asked him: "What are you doing master?" to which he replied: "I'm releasing the angel that I see trapped in this block of marble."

On the other hand, when David was going to face Goliath, he asked: *"What shall be done for the man who kills this Philistine and takes away the reproach from Israel?"* (1 Samuel 17:26).

It is interesting to note that before starting the fight David inquired about the reward he would receive for killing this giant. And he was so focused on the victory that the Lord was going to give him, that before confronting the giant he took five stones, instead of one.

According to some biblical scholars, Goliath had four brothers who were also giants. So, David, not only prepared himself to face Goliath but also his brothers, should it be necessary.

Therefore, if you have really decided to take your spiritual growth seriously, be ready to pay the price, you must overcome instability and focus.

Finally, I consider it useful to ask you the following questions:

What aspects of your life do you need to grow?

Of the things you do every day, what should you stop doing?

What are you not doing that you should do to be able to develop?

More than an option, our continuous growth, is the demand that has been established by the Lord, that the Lord requires of us.

*You did not choose Me, but **I chose you and appointed
you that you should go and bear fruit,** and that your
fruit should remain* (John 15:16).

Chapter 2

WE HAVE AN OWNER

Regarding our life, we are simple stewards;
the Lord is the true owner.

WE HAVE AN OWNER

*J*esus often made use of parables to illustrate deep and divine truths. The term parable comes from the Greek *parable,* which means comparison. Pointing out, that as it happens in one instance, so it also occurs in another.

Starting from this, we have some elements worthy of being considered in the parable of Luke 13:6, and that we will use as key principles to illustrate the way the Lord expects us to grow.

Among them:

The Fig Tree Had an Owner
The parable begins with the term, **"had"** which denotes ownership. Making it clear that the fig tree (which symbolizes our lives) is not owner of itself, but is someone's property.

Have you ever wondered why death does not give notice nor asks for permission to arrive? The reason is that life is not a possession, but a loan given to the human being, with an expiration date, whereas we are the stewards, but God is the true owner. And no owner asks permission to take what is his property, he just proceeds to take what is rightfully his. Concerning this, let's read the following Scriptures:

Then the Lord God **formed a man from the dust of the ground and breathed into his nostrils the breath of life,** *and the man became a living being* (Genesis 2:7 NIV).

Know that the Lord is God. **It is he who made us, and we are his;** *we are his people, the sheep of his pasture* (Psalm 100:3 NIV).

The Spirit of God has made me; *the breath of the Almighty gives me life* (Job 33:4 NIV).

That if you confess with your mouth **the Lord Jesus** *and believe in your heart that God has raised Him from the dead, you will be saved* (Romans 10:9).

The term "Lord" used in this last passage, comes from the Greek root *kurios* which means: supreme in authority, controller, sovereign and **absolute owner.**

Basically, this term alludes to **"had" us**, used at the beginning of the parable, that this verb comes from the Greek root word *sjeo* which means: hold, possess, condition, estimate, preserve, reign over, rebuke with rights.

So, considering this we can understand that our life is God's property because He sustains it, it belongs to Him, He conditions it, He gives it value, He conserves it, He reigns over it, and He reprimands it with rights.

Chapter 3

WE ARE NOT FROM THE WILD

*We have been planted and the one that
planted us was the vineyard expert.*

*A certain man had a fig tree planted
in his vineyard* (Luke 13:6).

WE ARE NOT FROM THE WILD

*T*he term "planted" comes from the Greek root *futeuo* which means to put a stem underground, so that it takes root and grows until it becomes a plant that produces the expected fruit.

I remember that when I was a little girl, my maternal grandmother, with whom I lived for a few years, in her desire to provide me with proper nutrition, told me:

—I want you to eat squash because it is good for you— to which I replied: —Grandma, I don't want it, you know I don't like squash.

She then said:

—I know you don't like it, but the one I prepared today is not like the others.

So, I asked her: —Why?— And she said, —because I planted and cultivated it myself, especially for you.

Her answer caught my attention not only because of what she said but because of how much she meant to me. I didn't want her work and dedication to be in vain. So, as soon as I sat down to eat, she explained:

—A few months ago, I found some seeds on the table of the squash vendor, I brought them home and planted them in the patio, and being underground for a while, they became plants and produced what I have prepared for you today with lots of love.

As for our comparison with the fig tree, it is interesting to see that scripture highlights the fact that it had also been planted. That is someone (in this case, the owner of the vineyard) wanted it to exist. Its existence was not of wild origin.

It should be noted that the production of wild plants occurs and grows spontaneously without the intervention of anyone. Meanwhile, the intentional production occurs, when someone takes seed in hand, understanding its potential, and plants it in the adequate soil, buries it to make it become a plant.

> *Although these dark and painful places seem like our doom, in heaven's eyes they are the ideal places for us to bloom.*

When my grandmother saw the seeds on the vendor's table, she intended to have a squash harvest from those seeds, and to attain that goal she had to bury them in the ground; underground, in darkness, where nobody saw them. While giving them the necessary care expecting them to emerge, not in the same form as when they were buried, but as a squash-producing-plant, which also brings within themselves an abundant amount of seeds.

Comparably, in God's desire to transform us from "seeds to plants," He allows us to go through certain stages that could seem dark and oppressive. Through seasons of life in where we think that we will not survive, where strong trials bring us down and we are discouraged by circumstances, and situations that go beyond our understanding.

However, all this is allowed by God to foster the environment that we need for growth. Although these dark and painful places seem like our doom, to heaven it is the ideal place for us to bloom. And in spite of the unpleasantness and discomfort these places can cause, it is where we should remain, because it is the ground that contains the nutrients that we need to grow.

No Exceptions Made

Regardless of the talents you have, the resources you own, the vehicle you drive, the house where you live, or the position that you have; at some point before you can become an inspiration to others you must be willing to go through seasons of pressure and darkness. Just like the seed that goes into the ground and that later emerges as a plant.

The harvest of squashes latent inside the seeds found by my grandmother would have never been revealed if they had stayed on the vendor's table. In the same way, to see the manifestation of the deposits of glory that the Lord has placed inside of you, He takes you to the "patio," because he knows that you have too much of His glory inside of you to leave you lying around the vendor's table.

And although sometimes, you might pray asking Him to shorten your process and get you out of the situation in which you find yourself under pressure, He does not do it. Because if He gets you out before your time, it will abort the mighty harvest that you'll receive after completing the process.

Chapter 4

THE PLACE IS CHOSEN BY THE OWNER

*The ground in which God planted you
contains the nutrients that you need to grow.*

THE PLACE IS CHOSEN BY THE OWNER

*T*he place where the fig tree was planted, was chosen, it was not fortuitous. This is evident, through the expression **"in his vineyard."**

The term **his** used in this passage comes from the Greek root word *idios* and means of private or separate use. This isn't just any vineyard, but a parcel of land explicitly chosen by the owner, according to his expert criteria.

The wine grower oversees preparing the vineyard and giving the necessary care for the fig tree to increase its production. And because of his knowledge and expertise, the wine grower knows that to get good results from a plantation, certain specific conditions must be met, such as:

Cleaning the Ground

Often, vineyards are planted on the outskirts of the hills. The land is cultivated with a hoe and shovel, commonly two types of stones are found; large and small.

I DARE YOU TO GROW

The small stones are left because they contribute with moisture retention and clear the soil, causing oxygen to penetrate in the roots so that these can spread into the deep zones which ensure the firmness and life of the plant.

However, large stones must be removed because they are a hindrance to the growth of the vines. In this process, the wine grower, based on his knowledge, decides which stones should be left and which ones should be removed. Regarding the condition of the land, where you were planted, the stones allied to your growth are conserved and those that threaten your growth, are removed by our "Expert Wine grower."

> *Because of his knowledge and expertise, the wine gorwer knows that to get good results from a plantation, certain specific conditions must be met.*

I accepted the Lord at the age of 16 while living in Long Island, an island on the East side of New York. I had everything that in human terms, a teenager could desire. I drove my own car; I had clothes that I wouldn't wear more than twice and made a lot of money for someone my age. I was awarded a scholarship for my university studies, among many other things. But when the time came to move towards what He had planned for me from eternity, instead of advancing, it seemed that my life was going backward.

A few months after I received Jesus as my Savior, the Lord allowed me to visit my native country, to where I migrated several years ago. There I met, and later married a man of limited resources, a pastor, a university student, with no possibilities of leaving the country with me, and who was also ten years older than me.

The people who were part of my environment, among them relatives, friends and church family said that this pastor did not qualify to be my husband. This was due to what was expected of the young woman who lived and developed an important part of her life in the United States. But even though he didn't have the adequate "profile" regarding advancement, this man had been chosen by God for me, according to His purposes.

> *When you ask God to reign in your life, He takes you seriously.*

At the time, no one understood this, when I painfully had to leave my home to go back to my native country, the Dominican Republic.

This event was very difficult for those around me (including myself). It was as if, in a cruel way, I had been stripped of everything I had (my mother, siblings, the church where I had been born spiritually, my job, the offers and opportunities I had, my friends, among many other things). But what seemed to be a loss, was God cleaning and preparing the ground of my life which resulted in what His grace has made us today.

Because of the way in which "well-off" was perceived, the people who loved me thought that I had to choose a husband of a certain wealth to be able to continue living the kind of lifestyle that I was used to. But when you allow God to rule your life, He takes you seriously, establishing His will above your wishes and the "good intentions" that others would have for you.

And because He is The King and not a president, His government is monarchical, not democratic. So, it does not require our vote, or that of any parliamentary committee, to execute His will.

Although my husband did not have a lot of material resources, God had deposited in Him the exact tools needed to prepare the ground of my life.

After years of preparation and training, the same God that took me out of the United States, brought me back, but no longer in the same way as I left. I was now a new version of me, which after going through everything I went through, I came to understand that well-being is not based on the possession of things, but that the Owner of all things possesses us for the fulfillment of His purposes on Earth.

The decision to reach the destiny that God designed for you must always be linked to your disposition to surrender to Him. Because in more than one occasion you will have to make great sacrifices, suffer certain "losses," let some people go, reject things that seem good, and take up other things that do not seem to be; this may (as in my case) be questioned by the people around you.

Many, not having the revelation of the destiny that God has outlined for you, will not understand it. We see this example in the life of the Patriarch Abraham, to whom after having received great promises, God said to him:

"Take your son, your only son, whom you love — *Isaac — and go to the region of Moriah. Sacrifice him there* *as a burnt offering on a mountain I will show you." Early* *the next morning Abraham got up and loaded his donkey.* *He took with him two of his servants and his son Isaac.* *When he had cut enough wood for the burnt offering, he set* *out for the place God had told him about.*

On the third day Abraham looked up and saw the place *in the distance.* **He said to his servants, "Stay here with** **the donkey while I and the boy go over there. We will** **worship and then we will come back to you"** (Genesis 22:2-5 NIV).

Notice that when Abraham was able to see the mount (the place of sacrifice), he asked the servants that accompanied him to stay and wait for his return. He did not take them with him because what was about to take place on the mount, was only between God, who asked for the sacrifice, and a man who was willing to surrender in obedience.

Genuine worship of God always involves an act of surrender. This is why Abraham said to his servants, that *he would go ahead with* *the boy to worship God* and ordered them to wait for him in the place where they were. Since God's promises to us are according to our destiny and according to the promises, are the tests and demands, therefore, the servants would have never been able to understand the request that God had

> *Genuine* *worship of* *God always* *involves an act* *of surrender.*

made to Abraham. God's purposes with the servants were not the same as His purposes with Abraham.

Similarly, according to the destiny that God has designed for you, the demands that He makes from you will be different from that of other people. Many, not understanding the cause, will question your level of commitment and willingness to obey. But do not let them stop you from taking your sacrifice to the mount. Be strong, give God your best and order the servants to just: WAIT FOR ME HERE!

Creating a place

On the other hand, before a space can be filled, it must first be emptied. And the story of Joseph, is one of the best examples. His name in Hebrew means "God adds." Something interesting when considering names in antiquity is that it alludes to the essence and destiny of someone. So, according to his name, Joseph was destined to receive great things. However, before this became a reality, he was exposed to certain circumstances that were completely contrary to the meaning of his name.

He was stripped of his adolescence, his home, support and protection of his father, the opportunity to live with his brothers, the coat his father had made him, his land, his culture, his reputation, and his freedom.

According to the human perspective, one can have the impression that Joseph had even lost significant years of his life. Since the time he arrived in Egypt, until the moment when he was taken out of prison, according to biblical records, thirteen years passed

(See Genesis 37:2, 39:1, 40 and 41:1). But what seemed as a waste of time, resources, and opportunities, was actually a preparation period necessary for Joseph to be able to handle the greatness that he was to receive later.

Therefore, when it seems that God is withholding something from you, it's not a loss. In reality, He is creating a space to position you for what is to come.

Chapter 5

WHAT YOU SOW WILL DETERMINE YOUR HARVEST

*Your existence is proof that this generation
needs something your life has to offer.*

WHAT YOU SOW WILL DETERMINE YOUR HARVEST

*A*nother step that the wine grower usually carries out, for the proper development of the vineyard, is to choose the seed to be sown, according to the type of fruit desired for the harvest. Planting a fig tree speaks directly of what is expected from the planting.

Before God created us, He placed inside of us the exact essence of what He expects in return. So, He will never demand something from us which He hasn't already given us.

Just as a builder first receives an idea, and then proceeds to make plans and later build, God completes His plans in us even before these become visible in the physical world.

When a builder prepares to begin construction, he knows beforehand the purpose of the building, and what it will be used for. Nobody starts building something without knowing its purpose. In the same manner, one does not plant a seed to wait and see what comes out fortuitously. The reason for the construction determines the shape of the building. The sowing done, determines the expected harvest and the way God made you, reveals His intention about the purpose He wanted to give you before you were born. For example, let's look at the Prophet Jeremiah:

"Before I formed you in the womb I knew you, before you were born I set you apart; I appointed you as a prophet to the nations."
"Alas, Sovereign Lord," I said, "I do not know how to speak; I am too young." But the Lord said to me, "Do not say, 'I am too young.' You must go to everyone I send you to and say whatever I command you (Jeremiah 1:5-7 NIV).

> **The reason for the construction determines the shape of the building. The sowing done, determines the expected harvest and the way God made you, reveals His intention about the purpose He wanted to give you before you were born.**

Notice that when God speaks to Jeremiah about how He would use his life, he resisted the call, arguing that he was very young to do the job. But the Lord only requested that he put to use the deposit He had made in him before birth. So, in response to such an argument, God responds *"...Do not say, 'I am too young.'"* By paraphrasing this, we can say that the Lord was saying to Jeremiah:

"You're not very young, you have been finished for years. Before I formed you in the womb, you already

existed in my mind; your parents had not yet joined when I designed you. I also sanctified you before you were born, before your mother felt the discomforts in her first months of pregnancy, you had already been sanctified. I took care of your mother's pregnancy so that you were not an abortive; I protected you while you were growing up.

I set you apart for my purposes; I had you in mind before you were born on Earth; I know you better than you do. I know what you are going to do before you do it; I know what you will say before you say it. You are mine, that is why you didn't fit into many groups and places, you were rejected by them because you do not belong in their sphere.

I ordained you as my minister; therefore, your credentials are eternal; you are an agent of mine, who came to earth with a specific mission. In my hand, you are a weapon of war. You have been chosen to fulfill the assignment I have given you because it bears your name. I formed you with the exact ability to deliver what I want you to give. Therefore, you will go where I send you, and say what I command".

In short, the Lord had chosen Jeremiah to be the voice from heaven in response to the decadence and deviation from spiritual principles in which the nation had fallen. Jeremiah was to fulfill the assignment for which God had designed him.

God inhabits eternity and knows the end from the beginning, even the things that have not yet occurred (See Isaiah 57:15). The way He made you; the moment for which He allowed you to be born; and the place where He positioned you, isn't mere chance. They are key indicators to understand the reason why you were born.

More than just simple human beings, we are the agents sent by God in response for the time, place and circumstances in which we have been positioned.

God Does Not Make Waste

Your existence is proof that this generation needs something you have to offer. What you are capable of doing is what God wants you to do. You have been created to satisfy the results that God expects for this time. Let's see this example:

> *More than just simple human beings, we're the agents sent by God in response for the time, place and circumstances in which we have been positioned.*

*Then the Lord said to Moses, "See, I have chosen Bezalel son of Uri, the son of Hur, of the tribe of Judah, **and I have filled him with the Spirit of God, with wisdom, with understanding, with knowledge and with all kinds of skills— to make artistic designs for work in gold, silver and bronze, to cut and set stones, to work in wood, and to engage in all kinds of crafts.** Moreover, I have appointed Oholiab son of Ahisamak, of the tribe of Dan, to help him. Also **I have given ability to all the skilled workers to make everything I have commanded you** (Exodus 31:1-6 NIV).*

Each of us has an assignment given by the Lord and to feel marked as people; it is necessary to put it to work.

Most people seek success based on superficial elements such as wealth, power, fame, luxury and prestige. They are instilled from an early age, that the goal in life is achieving material possessions, believing that the abundance of these is synonymous with success. However, no degree of realization can replace the satisfaction you receive in fulfilling the assignment that was given to you. The real key to success is to carry out what the Creator has assigned to you.

Chapter 6

CONSISTENT WITH THE RECORDS

That this which is written must still be accomplished in Me… For the things concerning Me have an end (Luke 22:37).

CONSISTENT WITH THE RECORDS

*I*n addition to cleaning the ground and selecting the specific type of seed to be planted, part of the vine grower's job is to keep a proper written record of what the harvest is expected to be according to the planting. In the same way, the Lord has written in His records, what He expects us to be according to what He already knows about us.

Concerning this, let's look at the following passages of the sacred text:

*"For **whom He foreknew, He also predestined to be conformed to the image of His Son,** that He might be the firstborn among many brethren"* (Romans 8:29).

*"Your eyes saw my unformed body; **all the days ordained for me were written in your book** before one of them came to be"* (Psalm 139:16 NIV).

*"**This is the one about whom it is written:** 'I will send my messenger ahead of you, who will prepare your way before you'"* (Mathew 11:10 NIV).

*"**It is written:** 'And he was numbered with the transgressors'; and **I tell you that this must be fulfilled**

in me. Yes, what is written about me is reaching its fulfillment" (Luke 22:37).

Your life, before God, is like a book that has already been written

The Lord desires so much for you to fulfill what is written about you, that He's been committed to delivering you out of everything that has sought to destroy you. He has not allowed you to die, He has strengthened you when you were weak, and He has brought you back to the right path whenever you have strayed away. When you recognize that you have failed and turned away from your wrong doings, God picks you up and transforms your failures into testimonies that will help to build others up.

> *When you recognize that you have failed and turn away from your wrong-doings, God picks you up and transforms your failures into testimonies that will help to build others up.*

On the other hand, what is written about you is in the book where God is the Author and you are the main character. And this, like the rest of the book, was written by chapters.

As the book lover that I am, I have noticed three particularities about books that significantly call my attention:

1. Long before it reaches the reader's hands, it was finished by the author.

2. Although all the chapters have already been written at the time the reader receives it, he must initiate its reading in chapter one.

3. Each chapter gives continuity to the other and to understand chapter three, usually the reader should have read one and two.

As an example, let us consider some exciting aspects of "the book" that God wrote about the great leader of the Old Testament, called Moses:

» When he was thrown into the river, as the result of persecution against the Hebrew children on the part of Pharaoh, God allowed it to be precisely the daughter of Pharaoh, who found him, took him in, and raised him in the palace of his persecutor.

» He was educated as a prince, and his development didn't stop there, but day by day it grew in the face of Pharaoh himself.

» After he grew up, for having killed an Egyptian he fled to Midian, a desert land located northeast of Mount Sinai. Where after living a life of privileges, he became his father-in-law Jethro's employee.

When considering the drastic changes that occurred in the life of Moses, we could think: What good did it do him to get forty years of abundance and to be educated at the highest levels, if he was going to be taken to the wilderness to look after sheep as a hired hand of another man? But God never makes mistakes, and just like Moses' life, and ours, everything was written in His record.

Those 40 years in the palace were part of what the Lord had planned for him, as well as the 40 years that he lived in the wilderness. Moses' training, before exercising his call, lasted a total of 80 years. All those experiences were necessary because what he learned in the palace, would be supplemented by what he learned in the desert.

At some point in the process, this may have been incomprehensible for Moses. After fulfilling the time established by God for him in the land of Midian, the Angel of the Lord appeared to him in the middle of a burning bush; this experience marked the beginning of the mission for which he had been called for a long time.

With this event, God gave continuity to the fulfillment of the promise He had made to Abraham hundreds of years ago when He told him:

> *The tests and difficulties that God allows us to go through, have an expiration date even before they reach us, and occur until the purpose for which they are permitted is fulfilled.*

"...*Know certainly that your descendants will be strangers in a land that is not theirs, and will serve them, and they will afflict them* **four hundred years** (Genesis 15:13).

That is to say, that the descendants of Abraham had not yet been born, and the time of this slavery had already been foretold.

In the same way, the processes and difficulties that God allows us to go through, have an expiration date long before they reach us, and remain until they have fulfilled the purpose for which they were allowed.

Therefore, when the time comes for the people of Israel to leave Egypt, the Lord reveals Himself to Moses saying:

"I am the God of your father – the God of Abraham, the God of Isaac, and the God of Jacob." And Moses hid his face, for he was afraid to look upon God. And the Lord said: "I have surely seen the oppression of My people who are in Egypt, and have heard their cry because of their taskmasters, for I know their sorrows. So I have come down to deliver them out of the hand of the Egyptians, and to bring them up from that land to a good and large land, to a land flowing with milk and honey, to the place of the Canaanites and the Hittites and the Amorites and the Perizzites and the Hivites and the Jebusites.

Now therefore, behold, the cry of the children of Israel has come to Me, and I have also seen the oppression with which the Egyptians oppress them. Come now, therefore, and I will send you to Pharaoh that you may bring My people, the children of Israel, out of Egypt." *But Moses said to God, "Who am I that I should go to Pharaoh, and that I should bring the children of Israel out of Egypt?" So He said,* ***"I will certainly be with you. And this shall be a sign to you that I have sent you: When you have brought the people out of Egypt, you shall serve God on this mountain"*** (Exodus 3:6-12).

Based on this, we can understand that nothing that happened in the life of Moses was wasted. The 40 years of palace education allowed him to learn the language, culture, and protocol of Egypt, which was used by God for the fulfillment of the plan He had with him. Among all those who inhabited the earth at that time, there was not one person with the education that Moses had to go before Pharaoh.

On the other hand, his 40 years in the desert were not unsuccessful, because, in that period of time, he received specialized training that he had not receive before, and that he would also need for the fulfillment of his mission.

Chapter 7

NOT IN VAIN

*Everything you have done so far
will be used by God to make you more
effective at your next level.*

NOT IN VAIN

 *D*uring his stay in Midian, Moses received essential lessons for the fulfillment of his call. God showed him great signs of His power; among them, the rod that turned into a serpent.

Then Moses answered and said, "But suppose they will not believe me or listen to my voice; suppose they say, 'The Lord has not appeared to you.'" So the Lord said to him,

"What is that in your hand?" He said, "A rod." And He said, "Cast it on the ground." So he cast it on the ground, and it became a serpent; and Moses fled from it. Then the Lord said to Moses, "Reach out your hand and take it by the tail" (and he reached out his hand and caught it, and it became a rod in his hand), *"that they may believe that the Lord God of their fathers, the God of Abraham, the God of Isaac, and the God of Jacob, has appeared to you"* (Exodus 4:1-5).

And later, already in Egypt:

So the Lord said to Moses: "See, I have made you as God to Pharaoh, and Aaron your brother shall be your prophet."

"When Pharaoh speaks to you, saying, 'Show a

miracle for yourselves,' then you shall say to Aaron, 'Take your rod and cast it before Pharaoh, and let it become a serpent.'" So Moses and Aaron went in to Pharaoh, and they did so, just as the Lord commanded. And Aaron cast down his rod before Pharaoh and before his servants, and it became a serpent. But Pharaoh also called the wise men and the sorcerers; so the magicians of Egypt, they also did in like manner with their enchantments. For every man threw down his rod, and they became serpents. But Aaron's rod swallowed up their rods (Exodus 7:1, 9-12).

Pharaoh knew that Moses had not received this kind of training at his palace and probably when he understood the situation, he asked himself: Where did he learn this? We did not teach these tricks to Moses when he was here. And Moses did not receive that kind of training while in the palace; but he learned it at the specialized training "center" called the desert.

So, like Moses, we won't be completely ready to be used by the Lord until we have gone through this "center," and although our stay there could turn out to be uncomfortable and difficult, because apart from being an arid and inhospitable place, and at times vipers and other vermin will try to get you poisoned instead of training you, so do not take their poison. Activate the antidote that God has put inside of you, which will always be much stronger than the venom they spew.

The Authority of the Graduates

When Moses left Midian, he was not the same man that he was when he arrived. Because aside from the fact that his perspective changed, due to what had been revealed to him there, he also received the authority to be able to say:

"In the middle of the desert, I learned to depend on God, to wait on His defense, to trust in His promises and to understand that everything works for good, although at the moment it does not seem that way."

His experiences had enabled him to say to the people:

"Bundle up well, because the nights here are cold. Do not drink of certain waters because they are bitter. Be careful, because in this type of terrain some beasts and vipers may be roaming. "And if the people asked him, How do you know? He would answer:

"Because before bringing you, I had already been here."

So, after we go through the desert, we become much more efficient in fulfilling God's calling in our life.

Regarding this, the apostle Paul said:

*I know what it is to be in need, and I know what it is to have plenty. **I have learned the secret of being content in any and every situation,** whether well fed or hungry, whether living in plenty or in want* (Philippians 4:12 NIV).

The Lord does not train his agents for nothing. No matter what the circumstance you are going through, adopt the right attitude, give the best of yourself and learn from it.

Because everything you are learning through your circumstances will be used by God to make you more efficient at the next level you will be taken to.

If they don't know the story, they won't sense the glory

As you read a book, one chapter gives continuity to the next; God wrote your life's story in a book format, with new chapters for every stage. Therefore, when people come to you in your harvest chapter and they have not read the previous ones; they think that your story started where you are at now.

> *The Lord does not train his agents for nothing. So, no matter what the circumstance you are going through, adopt the right attitude, give the best of yourself and learn from it.*

They are bothered by the car you have, ignoring that there was a time when you depended on another person to get to where you wanted to go.

It bothers them to see the clothes you wear, not knowing that there was a time when everything you wore was borrowed, or at best, your purchases were of second, third or even fourth-hand nature.

They can't get over the fact of seeing where you live now, simply because they just don't know about the time when you had to live in someone else's home because your income was not enough to rent your own place.

They are hugely offended at seeing you in the position the Lord has put you; because they were not with you when God was forming your roots when you were invisible, when instead of being elevated and noticeable you were oppressed and pushed down.

They came to know you in the harvest chapter, they were not in the previous chapters, they think that what you have now, was obtained very quickly or even worse, someone handed it to you by favoritism. But before you face this, do not react, do not let yourself be provoked. Save time and don't waste efforts, because those that were absent at the time of your sowing won't understand the reasons for your harvest.

Chapter 8

COMING FOR THE FRUITS

*...He came seeking fruit on it
and found none* (Luke 13:6b).

COMING FOR THE FRUITS

*T*he cleaning of the ground, the selection of the seed and keeping records, are all part of the care efforts made by the wine grower to cultivate the fig tree. So, it is entirely understandable that he has expectations for the fruit it should yield.

The term "seek," used in the parable, comes from the Greek root word: *"zeteo"* which means to ask, want, require and demand. Nobody knows better how the harvest should turn out, than the one who sowed the seed. The owner of the fig tree expected to receive figs from it, because this is what he had sown.

In this sense, God is the one who planted us, and He knows exactly what we can bear. He does not require more than we can produce but does not settle for less. And it is because of what He knows about you and not the perception that you have about yourself, that sometimes He prepares situations where you can withdraw the deposits that He has placed inside of you.

What Do You Have in Your Hand?

Preparing to speak for a Women's Congress, at the time of being introduced by the pastor, a sister intervened, and with a firm voice said: "Pastor, I know that the service is being turned over to the speaker, but there is a testimony that I would like to share." The pastor looked at me and asked if I would give the opportunity to the sister. Without thinking twice, I immediately agreed.

> *God is the one who planted us, and He knows exactly what we can bear. He does not require more than we can produce but does not settle for less.*

The sister began to move towards the altar with a face of triumph, joy, and taking the microphone with a revived voice said: "Glory to God for this opportunity! I want to tell you that today, precisely one year ago, I was fired from the company I worked for over ten years. I remember when they gave me the unexpected notice of my dismissal; I felt a great concern and a deep sadness, so I asked God: "Lord, how do I support my family? You know I don't receive help from anyone, I'm a single mother, and I don't have another income."

But still, on my knees, the God that hears His children's prayers spoke to me and showed me what at first sight I didn't see. I listened to His voice in my spirit saying:

—Dear daughter, what do you have in your hand?— to which I answered: —I have nothing. My hands are empty.

According to the sister's testimony, the Lord said to her:

—No, your hands are not empty. Take a good look and tell me what you have in your hands.— Then she replied: —I only have five fingers in each hand.

—What else do you have?— the Lord insisted.

—An old 1989 deteriorated vehicle— answered the sister.

So once again the Lord spoke to her saying:

—And what do you know and like to do?

—I enjoy cooking a lot, Lord—, she answered.

—It was then that my eyes were opened—, she continued. —God helped me see that although I no longer had my former job, there was something that He had given me that I needed to put into action. It was my ability in the kitchen. I had to work with my hands, to obtain the desired result (food), which I was going to mobilize with my vehicle to the place where I had been fired, which from that time onward became my first marketplace.

Focus on what you have and not on what you need. When we use what we have, we begin to attract what we need.

"And today I wanted to give this testimony as in gratitude to the Lord because that's how I started with my own food sales company. In just one year, I have made almost 25% of what I made in 10 years working at my former employer. So, the Lord used the fact that I was fired to help me create my own business."

When we finished hearing the sister, we all applauded to the Lord, the One who does things well.

Just like the Lord did with this sister, the Lord has provided all of us with something that we can put to work. Focus on what you *have* and not on what you *need*. When we use what we *have*, we begin to attract what we *need*.

The twenty-sixth President of the United States, Theodore Roosevelt once said: *"Do what you can, with what you have, where you are."*

One of the leading causes of stagnation in many people is that they focus too much on what they can't do instead of seeing what they can do and visualize what has been provided to them. Let's look at these examples:

A certain woman of the wives of the sons of the prophets cried out to Elisha, saying, "Your servant my husband is dead, and you know that your servant feared the Lord. And the creditor is coming to take my two sons to be his slaves." **So Elisha said to her, "What shall I do for you? Tell me, what do you have in the house?" And she said, "Your maidservant has nothing in the house but a jar of oil."** *Then he said, "Go, borrow vessels from everywhere, from all your neighbors — empty vessels; do not gather just a few. And when you have come in, you shall shut the door behind you and your sons; then pour it into all those vessels, and set aside the full ones"* (2 Kings 4:1-4).

Although what the widow had seemed very little, the prophet gave her the order to multiply. The provision of abundance that she needed would come from putting to multiply what little she had.

On the other hand, in one of the clashes that

Samson had with the Philistines, the Bible tells us the following:

"He found a fresh jawbone of a donkey, reached out his hand and took it, and killed a thousand men with it. Then Samson said: "With the jawbone of a donkey, heaps upon heaps, With the jawbone of a donkey I have slain a thousand men!" (Judges 15:15-16).

The ideal weapon for this type of fight (according to human logic) would have been a sword, a spear, a javelin or an arrow. But the fact that Samson did not have any of these did not prevent him from carrying out the confrontation. So, without stopping to think about what he didn't have, he took what he had at hand (a simple donkey jaw), which in his hand became a weapon of mass destruction to defeat his enemies.

What about you, what do you have in your hand?

Chapter 9

DON'T LET FEAR HOLD YOU BACK

*Feeling fear in front of certain challenges
and demands of life is inevitable,
but letting it control us is unacceptable.*

DON'T LET FEAR HOLD YOU BACK

*F*ear is a silent enemy that comes into your life to create doubt and prevent you from conquering what God has for you. Feeling fear in front of certain challenges and demands of life is inevitable, but letting it control us is unacceptable. Let's see this example:

"*Then he who had received the one talent came and said, 'Lord, I knew you to be a hard man, reaping where you have not sown, and gathering where you have not scattered seed. And* **I was afraid, and went and hid your talent in the ground.** *Look, there you have what is yours.' But his lord answered and said to him, 'You wicked and lazy servant, you knew that I reap where I have not sown, and gather where I have not scattered seed. So you ought to have deposited my money with the bankers, and at my coming I would have received back my own with interest. Therefore take the talent from him, and give it to him who has ten talents. For to everyone who has, more will be given, and he will have abundance; but from him who does not have, even what he has will be taken away*" (Matthew 25:24-29).

It's interesting to see how the man of the parable buried the talent he received, instead of burying the fear that held him back. And the reason (according to him) is that he didn't want to get into trouble. The man ignored that inevitably, growth usually brings problems. Which means that if you don't want problems, you don't want growth. If we are to become everything that God wants us to be, there will also be a high cost to pay, but not reaching our God given goal will cost us even more.

> *Growth usually brings problems. Which means that if you don't want problems, you don't want growth.*

How to stop fear from holding us back?

The way to stop fear from holding us back is responding to it in the right way.

Barriers created by fear, often manifest through the following statements:

› *I don't know how to do it:*

One of the strategies of the enemy is to make you believe that you are incapable of bringing out that which has been deposited inside of you.

Even if your performance isn't the best at the beginning, don't give up doing what has been assigned to you; remember that everyone that does something right today is because they have learned from their past mistakes, and did not allow themselves to be overcome by their failures.

"The proactive approach to a mistake is to acknowledge it, correct and learn from it. This literally turns a failure into a rich learning experience. It is not what others do or our own mistakes that hurt us the most; it is our response. Our response to any error affects the quality of the next moment, it is important to immediately admit and correct our mistakes so they do not have power over that next moment." Stephen R. Covey.

Do not fear making mistakes, fear only the absence of a creative, constructive and corrective response to these.

Oprah Winfrey once said that a television producer qualified her as "not fit for TV" after making several mistakes during an audition. And ignoring what the woman said, she decided to improve by putting herself on a growth track to become better at what she did.

> *Don't be fearful of making mistakes, but do fear the absence of a creative, constructive and corrective response when facing them.*

Today, Oprah is a producer and presenter of her own television show, actress, businesswoman, philanthropist, and an American book critic; with the financial wealth to buy the TV station where her program airs, the same channel where she was rejected from in her early years.

› *I have too many problems:*

Before God created you, He knew all the battles you would face and prepared you so that (if you choose) you could move forward. Don't expect to be problem-free to do the things you should. Solomon wrote:

He who observes the wind will not sow, And he who regards the clouds will not reap (Ecclesiastes 11:4).

Once I read a story about two fishermen who were lost in the middle of a lake. The storm was blowing so intensely that they couldn't see anything. Then, one fisherman told his partner: "We have two options, we can pray, or we can paddle. Which one do you think we should do?" To which his partner replied: "We will pray, while we paddle."

Don't let the storms of life stop you, keep paddling, while things are being resolved.

> *Sometimes God expects us to act out of obedience and not because of how we feel.*

› I feel too tired:

Sometimes God expects us to act out of obedience and not because of how we feel.

Don't expect to feel your "best" to start advancing.

The Lord will strengthen you as you begin to move forward. Let's see this example:

"Now it happened as He went to Jerusalem that He passed through the midst of Samaria and Galilee. Then as He entered a certain village, there met Him ten men who were lepers, who stood afar off. And they lifted up their voices and said, "Jesus, Master, have mercy on us!"

So when He saw them, He said to them, "Go, show yourselves to the priests." **And so it was that as they went, they were cleansed** (Luke 17:11-14).

This story receives special attention when we

consider that the Law says that a leper can only come before a priest when he or she has been healed of leprosy (See Leviticus 14). Something to consider is that Jesus could've healed them immediately, but instead asked them to go show themselves as healed people to the priests, even before they were able to confirm the healing. The lepers knew the implications of showing themselves unclean before the priests, but despite their reasoning they obeyed the order given by the Lord.

And as they walked, diseased with leprosy, towards the place where they had to present themselves healed, as they went, they were made whole.

› *My time has passed:*

The expiration date of a product, according to the manufacturer, indicates that the life cycle of the product has reached its end. The date is established before putting the product on the market, according to what the manufacturer determined that the product contains.

> *One of the most important goals of our life should be not to waste a single moment of our existence.*

In the same way, before we were born, God set a date for the end of our days on Earth. Our time on the planet starts with our birth and ends when our lungs stop breathing. Therefore, the fact that you are reading this book confirms that you are alive; and if you are still alive it is because your time is not over yet.

There are things you still need to do, places you must go, people you should know, experiences you must acquire. Your "time" was not just when you were an adolescent or a youth, or the time in which you were in a certain position.

Your time is the whole season in which you have lived, so don't jump ahead of time to your expiration date.

In this regard, I have noticed that many people get confused when they come to the end of a given season in life. But it should be noted that the end of a season always marks the beginning of another, and the closing of a season makes room for a next one.

Just as failures give us the opportunity to start again more intelligently, the end of one season allows us to start another with experiences that we didn't have before.

In fact, one of the strategies used in human resources in past decades is the creation of teams made up of people that have retired from companies to serve as advisors to new company associates.

One of the most important goals of our life should be not to waste a single moment of our existence. And make the words of the psalmist our confession:

I will sing to the Lord **as long as I live.** *I will praise my God* **to my last breath!** (Psalm 104:33 NLT).

Chapter 10

MULTIPLY YOURSELF IN OTHERS

*Teaching others what you have learned
prepares you to be promoted.*

MULTIPLY YOURSELF IN OTHERS

*A*nother way to put into production what has been given to us is to teach others what we know, and it is essential that we do it because God will demand what he has entrusted to us, plus interest.

The gift that has been given to you becomes more useful when you use it to contribute to the activation of the gift of others. Remember, what you have received is not your private property, it was given to you by God to serve as a blessing in the lives of others.

On one occasion, while I was praying, I felt a great concern and a strong commitment to contribute to the development of others, especially those who needed some guidance to begin their growth. About that time, I had just finished a few personal projects, so I felt the responsibility to share with others what the Lord had allowed me to learn.

Right there, I understood that this, more than a simple desire, was something that the Lord required me to do, so I asked Him how exactly did I have to do this. He spoke to my heart and said:

"I want you to dedicate one day a week to multiply in others what I have allowed you to receive."

In obedience to this call, we began a christian school of leadership in which the first three years of its running it produced:

» Teachers
» Preachers
» Intercession and deliverance ministries
» Project management and christian events ministries
» Social and community assistance ministries
» And the certification of more than 140 leaders

All these leaders were from different churches, who later became responsible for imparting what they had received in the lives of others. Among them, some teachers gave continuity to this design at the local level, as God opened doors for us to expand a vision for advancement and growth in other places, inside and outside the border of our nation.

> *If you don't share with others what you have received, it won't matter how powerful it may be; it will have a limited reach.*

At the time of writing this book, we are getting ready to start a new ministry training project, which would go into all Latin America and the Spanish-speaking communities in the United States. In the same way, I urge you to convey to others everything you have learned. If you don't share with others what you have received, it won't matter how powerful it may be; it will have a limited reach.

Don't just pass through other people's lives, help them to improve

An improver is someone who has the ability to take something or someone to a higher level than before. To be an improver, you must understand that regardless of the current conditions, everyone can become much better. This point is particularly important because if we do not think that something can be improved, we will not be able to put effort into making it better.

On the other hand, we must understand that this process requires time and effort. Investing in people will never involve a loss. On the contrary, it represents one of the greatest legacies we can make to our generation.

In the Bible, we find multiple examples of men and women who were improvers, as is the case of David, who was in the cave of Adullam, which means: "a closed place." He trained, polished and fashioned a group of men who were wounded, in mourning, indebted and bitter. He led them from that condition to become a mighty army, which came to be known as David's mighty warriors.

It's easy to recognize someone's talent when it is already blossomed, but there is a greater need for people who can see the gift beforehand and contribute to its flourishing.

It is interesting to notice the fact that neither the

closed place nor the circumstances in which they were in, prevented David from working to improve and train these men (See 1 Samuel 22:1-2).

Contribute to the growth of others and the Lord will reward you.

It is easy to recognize someone's talent when it is already blossomed, but there is a greater need for people who can see the gift beforehand and contribute to its flourishing.

An improver is someone who takes something good out of the bad and brings something extraordinary out of the ordinary. The difference between the ordinary and the extraordinary is the prefix "extra" that implies adding to the ordinary: extra time, extra effort, extra dedication, extra knowledge and extra money.

If what is around you is not good, it is because God wants to use you to improve it. Everything that passes through your life should be better than it was before it came to you.

Chapter 11

DIG OUT UNFRUITFULNESS

But he answered and said to him,
'Sir, let it alone this year also, until I dig
around it and fertilize it (Luke 13:8).

DIG OUT UNFRUITFULNESS

*I*n the core of the passage, we are presented with a decisive dialogue between the owner of the fig tree and the wine grower who takes care of it, representing the interaction between the Father and our mediator, the Son, Jesus Christ.

The owner of the fig tree had been seeking fruit for three consecutive years, symbolizing three harvest seasons in which it had produced nothing. For which it was only reasonable to cut it down. And based on the facts, the owner said: cut it down! In the Greek, this word is *"ekkopto"* and is translated, to frustrate or cut down.

But the wine grower intervened and based on mercy, (although it was just to cut down the fig tree, because of its continuing unfruitfulness), he says to the owner: *"Let it alone this year also, **until I dig around it and fertilize it,** and if it bears fruit, well. But if not, after that you can cut it down."*

The term "dig" used in this passage, comes from the Greek root word *"skapto"* which translated is: to dig out, excavate like with a hoe.

This reveals to us that in his attempt to make the fig tree produce, the wine grower will dig out everything from the tree that makes it unfruitful.

In like manner, due to His desire to make us productive, God causes certain remorse to take place in our lives. Some of these include:

Bad actions

The Lord loves us so much that He will work in different ways to get everything out of our lives that prevent us from bearing the fruit that He expects. And just like the term dig, is translated: "to dig out, excavate like with a hoe," this implies that even buried weeds, that at first sight can't be seen, they will be removed; God will remove everything that eats away our productivity.

> *If you have unresolved issues in the spiritual world, your fruitfulness will never be at its best until you settle the situation.*

› Hidden sins produce world, your unfruitfulness

Even if you don't tell anyone, or you don't want it to be known, hiding the evidence of your sin by erasing your call history, undoing your messages or deleting your search history on the internet, if you don't admit to your wrongdoing, if you do not repent and depart, everything will come to light. And this will be the way the Lord will use to heal you.

If you have unresolved issues in the spiritual world, your fruitfulness will never be at its best until you settle the situation.

If you know that what you are doing is not right, if there is sin delaying your growth, instead of holding on to it or justifying the reasons why you do it, take a "spiritual hoe," go to the Holy Spirit, and in the name of Jesus, cut it out!

*"Come now, and **let us reason together**," Says the Lord, "Though your sins are like scarlet, they shall be as white as snow; though they are red like crimson, they shall be as wool* (Isaiah 1:18).

Whoever conceals their sins does not prosper, *but the one who confesses and renounces them finds mercy* (Proverbs 28:13 NIV).

Bad company

Whenever God wants to bless you, He will send people to do it. But in the same way, whenever the devil seeks to destroy you, he will also send people. Satan is cunning, and as far as offers are concerned, he works from three realms that include: your shortcomings, what you want, and what you like.

> *Doing the wrong thing, for the right reason means that evil becomes good.*

› Bad company because of lack

The enemy uses your needs to employ deceptive tricks, making you believe that having a particular person (that you know is not the right one), isn't that bad after all because you "need it." However, the

Bible says:

*...For **your Father knows** what you need...* (Matthew 6:8).

God knows everything that we need, including our need for affection. He understands very well every one of our situations and knows that occasionally we feel alone. But the fact of needing something does not give us the right to acquire it the wrong way. Doing the wrong thing, for the right reason does not mean that evil becomes good.

Let's look at this example of an unemployed father saying: "I don't know how I'm going to feed my children, but I won't let them go hungry." This is a valid concern from a father that feels for his children, and they certainly need to be fed, and the father must provide for their nutrition. Nevertheless, this does not give this father the right to deceive, assault or mug someone just because he has a genuine need. And if he does the same, for reasons other than his own, he will pay in the same way as those people.

› *Bad company we want*

Everything your heart desires, if it is within God's plans for you, will come at the right time. And if it is not within His plans for you, it does not matter how you obtain it, it will not bless you.

The blessing of the Lord makes one rich, and He adds no sorrow with it (Proverbs 10:22).

On the other hand, there are also people that the Lord could remove from our lives, not necessarily because they are evil, but because the time of their assignment in our lives has come to an end. And although it was good to have them in our life for a season, the time has come for them to leave. We should ask the Lord to help us to understand when someone who has been with us for a season, must move on. If God has taken them out, don't insist on bringing them back. If the Lord wanted to cut them off from you, don't try to make amends, and if the relationship is dead don't try to revive it.

> *If God has taken them out, don't insist on bringing them back. If the Lord wanted to cut them off from you, don't try to make amends, and if the relationship is dead don't try to revive it.*

›*Bad company that we like*

Like, is another hook that the enemy will use to tempt us; he is very cunning and knows that if we do not like his offer, he won't succeed in his attempt to make us fall in his trap. But the fact that we like it, does not legalize that we be linked to people who attempt against our good relationship with the Lord. This is what the Bible says regarding this:

I say then: Walk in the Spirit, and **you shall not fulfill the lust of the flesh.** *For the flesh lusts against the Spirit, and the Spirit against the flesh; and these are contrary to one another, so that you do not do the things that you wish* (Galatians 5:16-17).

Bad habits

The Lord also expects us to make use of the "hoe" to work with our bad habits.

A habit is defined as a behavior that repeats regularly. There are good habits that generate discipline, and there are bad habits that take us nowhere; but numb us, waste our time and affect our production capacity. These bad habits enter slowly and subtly, and they settle in us producing not just negative results but frustration as well.

When we minimize what we do wrong, these bad habits end up controlling us. Some people say: "If I just do this occasionally it is no big deal, it is just a little lie, it is nothing, etc." However, it would be good to remember that Adam and Eve ate **once** of the forbidden fruit, that Ananias and Sapphira lied **once,** and that Moses struck the rock **only once.**

> *If you want to eliminate negative habits, replace them with positive habits.*

If you want to eliminate negative habits, replace them with positive habits. Like the Apostle Paul declares in Ephesians 4:25-32:

"...Putting away lying, let each one of you speak truth, let him who stole steal no longer, but rather let him labor, working with his hands what is good...

Let all bitterness, wrath, anger, clamor, and evil speaking be put away from you, with all malice. And be kind to one another..."

On the other hand, according to some studies made on human behavior, for something to become a habit or part of a routine practice, a person must go from 21 days to 6 weeks doing the same thing. So, if for six weeks you set the alarm to wake up at 5:00 in the morning, (as mentioned above) after having done this for a time, even if you don't use the alarm, it will be habitual for you to wake up every day at that time. Based on this, it would be beneficial to set a 6-week practice for some of our actions to become habitual. They would turn us 180° degrees toward success! I encourage you to try it out.

Chapter 12

YOU WILL BE FERTILIZED

*Don't use a different description for
that which Heaven calls a fertilizer.*

YOU WILL BE FERTILIZED

*T*he use of the fertilizer is also part of the wine growers strategy to make the fig tree produce.

The term fertilize, used in this passage, comes from the Greek root *"kopria"* which is translated as manure.

Something that makes sense when we remember that fertilizer, is the manure placed in the portion of ground or on a plant connected to it, to make it more fertile and fruitful; it is made from waste, dung and other organic material.

Both garbage and manure are disposable and malodorous elements. But this interesting mixture, the wine grower considers useful to cultivate the fig tree.

Consider the importance of fertilizer in this parable; it helps us understand the usefulness of the processes that enter our lives as "stinky waste," that exposes us. God does not ask for permission nor does He consult with us, because if we had an option, we would flat out reject it. However, the Lord will never allow us to go through any of this if it weren't for his kind intentions to fertilize us.

If you pause and think for a moment, the experiences that have brought you to a higher level of growth, are precisely the most unpleasant ones. In other words, the ones that came in with more "fertilizer."

I remember when I arrived in the Dominican Republic, to marry my husband. Some of the people from the church he pastored rejected me at first sight because they said that (according to what they could see) I didn't have a calling from God, I was not a woman of ministry, and if my husband married me he would have to carry the cross of living with a woman who had nothing to contribute to his ministry.

Among those people, was a woman that many considered to be the prophet of the house, who during a Sunday service asked my husband for an opportunity to tell him in front of all those present: "Pastor, the wife you have chosen was not the one God had for you. He was going to give you a woman of ministry, a pastor, and preacher; but you chose wrong because this one, does not know how to speak."

> *But what God has said about you, is over and above what others can see or think about you.*

But what God has said about you, is over and above what others can see or think about you. Probably, as you read this, you realize that you have never had to go through something like this, and perhaps you wouldn't be interested in going through it either.

But in my case, God didn't seek my opinion about this situation, and I'm thankful for that. Only to think how cruel and daring that rejection would be, I would have probably asked him to not to let me go through something so humiliating, shameful and depressing.

But that which I have defined was considered by Heaven, as a portion of "fertilizer." Something that would initiate in me the process of growth, which continues to this day.

That night, after such experience, I came to the house, entered the room, and behind closed doors, I cried out to God and asked Him: Why did you bring me here? To have others humiliate me in that way? Doesn't it hurt you that they do this to me, don't you care?

Desperate for an answer, I tuned into the radio station that I usually listen. A prophet of the Lord was on, and by the Spirit of God declared: "Right now, in San Francisco de Macoris, in the Dominican Republic, there is a young woman on her knees, asking God: 'Why did you bring me here to make me go through this? Do you not care what I'm going through, Lord?' But to you, young woman, listening to me, this is what the Lord says to you: "Dry your tears, get up from the floor and declare yourself in victory. It was God, who took you there to awake in you, what he had given to you before you were born." And to this, the prophet added: "It was the Lord who took you to the place that you are now to make you grow and mature because you will be an instrument in His hands to take His message across the island and then to the nations."

Upon receiving those powerful words, my sadness

disappeared, my perspective changed, and I felt like my strength was increased like that of the buffalo. From that moment on, I just wanted to grow and please God in the place that He had planted me.

At that time, I wanted to enroll in the university, but as part of His strategy, the Lord had me do high school again. That is to say, that I had to redo the four years of high school that I had completed in the United States.

Something that I saw as a delay, but God extraordinarily used my husband to help me see, that if He allowed it, it was for the purpose to achieve something, and indeed it was. Because I had to do presentations continuously, I improved my fluidity and communication skills which I didn't have when I arrived in the country. In addition, I developed a strong habit of prayer, fasting and Bible reading, which I believe was the most significant trigger to begin the fulfillment of what God had said was going to happen.

After about a year, everyone started to see changes in me, and was amazed at what God was doing; they would tell me: "Wow, you have grown, you don't look anything like when you arrived, you have surprised us!" However, that which was a surprise for them, was never to God, because He knew the exact deposits He had put inside of me.

Years later, the same woman who had said that I had no ministry, invited me several times to preach at congresses and other activities that she conducts, in which many times she has apologized for not having perceived, from the beginning, what the Lord had entrusted to me. But while she apologizes, I always interrupt her saying: "Please, don't apologize, you were just the person who delivered the fertilizer that I needed to grow and become what the Lord wanted me to be."

Maybe you have also been rejected in some way, perhaps some people have told you that you are not cut out for ministry, that you don't qualify for certain things, that you won't amount to anything. Others who could've possibly opened a door for you, have closed them, trying to stop your growth. But I can assure you, that all this has been allowed by the One who planted you, not to harm you, but to "fertilize" you.

Therefore, don't resent people that attack you. They are not doing it because they want to, but because they have been assigned. So, treat them well, bless them, buy them a gift if you can. They are not at war with you; they are just fertilizing you; not harming you. They are helping you to wake up; they are not blocking you but stimulating you to bear good fruit, even those that you would never think you could produce.

PART TWO

GROWING LIKE PALM TREES

Chapter 13

DEEP ROOTS TO STAND STRONG

The righteous shall flourish like a palm tree.
(Psalm 92:12).

DEEP ROOTS TO STAND STRONG

*T*he palm tree is a slender tree with a rough trunk that can measure up to 30 meters high.

Its lifetime is approximately 200 years, and it is considered a symbol of triumph and conquest in some nations. Different findings of the palm tree have revealed that it grows better under climate and terrain pressure. The more challenging its environment, the better it develops.

The fact that the palm tree grows in tropical and arid grounds causes it to deepen its roots up to 300 meters, causing it to be up to 10 times deeper than high. This condition allows it to be battered by winds and storms, and even if bent and shaken, no storm can pluck it from the ground where it was planted.

The importance of having a foundation

For any structure to be stable, undoubtedly, it must have a firm foundation.

The stability of any building, no matter its height, will depend on the depth and solidity of its foundation.

It is not common to hear people say: "Wow, that tree has deep roots!" or, "What a strong cornerstone does that building have!" And the reason is that the foundations of a structure can't be appreciated at a glance. It is precisely what we do not see, that sustains the aspects that we see when we look at the greatness, amplitude and height of the structure.

> *The stability of any building, no matter its height, will depend on the depth and solidity of its foundation.*

Therefore, before we can rise to higher levels, God will first work to create in us, the adequate foundations.

*Now I say that **the heir, as long as he is a child,** does not differ at all from a slave, though he is master of all, **but is under guardians and stewards until the time appointed by the father** (Galatians 4:1-2).*

At times, the kindness of a parent towards a child manifests itself through the denial of things that are not bad for the child, but the timing isn't right for the child to have them. For example, if an eight-year-old asks for the car keys to go to the store, the parent's kindness, at that time, will be manifested by denying the request. At that age, it would present a grave risk to the life of the child.

However, if at the age of eighteen, after obtaining his/her driver's license, the child makes the same request, the same kindness that made the parent deny the car at eight years of age, will grant the request at the age of eighteen.

Note, that in this example I am talking about the

same parent, the same child and the same request. The only differentiating factor is timing. The car that blesses your son at eighteen, could kill him at eight years old. It would be inappropriate for a parent to give a child something beneficial outside the adequate timing.

Everything that God has prepared for you is ready

"Eye has not seen, nor ear heard, nor have entered into the heart of man the things which God has prepared for those who love Him (1 Corinthians 2:9).

The Lord is not preparing to give you a blessing, He is preparing you to receive it; He is working inside of you so that you have a deep enough root system to sustain you in the level to which you will be taken.

> *The Lord is not preparing to give you a blessing, He is preparing you to receive it; He is working inside of you so that you have a deep enough root system to sustain you in the level to which you will be taken.*

That's why when you skip the processes that are part of building your foundation, God ensures that in some way you have to go through them again.

Because if you do not respond, according to God's expectations, the trials He sends through Carlos (for a name's sake) He will repeat it with Edward, it is about you. God is working in you and they are only instruments that the Lord is using to strengthen your foundation and lead you into maturity.

Even though our interests are focused on rising quickly, God's interests are focused on our solid growth. We can only succeed in our path to growth by taking consistent steps and not quick jumps.

The steps of a good man are ordered by the Lord, and He delights in his way (Psalm 37:23).

Even Jesus took steps and didn't jump. On one occasion, they tried to crown Him before crucifying him, and He did not allow it, because He was not willing to skip any step.

> **We can only succeed in our path to growth by taking consistent steps and not quick jumps.**

*Then those men, when they had seen the sign that Jesus did, said, "This is truly the Prophet who is to come into the world." Therefore when **Jesus** perceived that they were about to come and take Him by force to make Him king, He departed again to the mountain by Himself alone* (John 6:14-15).

His coronation would come after his crucifixion and not before.

But we see Jesus... crowned with glory and honor, that He, by the grace of God, might taste death for everyone (Hebrews 2:9).

It is the agony that brings the oasis; the disease that opens a path to health, and poverty that makes you value prosperity. Each season that you go through prepares you for the next level to which you will rise.

Therefore, don't wait to reach the end of the journey to thank the Lord, praise Him on every step of the way, because He will grow your roots through these things.

Foundation Process in Action

When you don't understand your foundation process, Satan takes advantage of this to make you believe that you are not advancing. And even if you are not yet at the levels the Lord has promised you, you are not at the same place where you started. Your advancement hasn't stopped, it is just that your roots have been expanding.

So, in the middle of this process, don't despair, or make any hasty decisions that could alter your destiny. Hold on to the promises of the One who called you, because He won't leave His work incomplete. Your foundation process will come to its finalization.

> *So, no matter what you are going through now, just make sure you are in the place where God wants you and that you do what He commanded you to do. The rest is up to the Lord*

When Job was tested and suffered the loss of his children, house, sheep, cattle and everything he had, he said: But He (God) knows the way that I take; when He has tested me, I shall come forth as gold (Job 23:10).

In God's agenda, there is an appointed time for each of the processes we go through. Let's see these examples:

And Zacharias said to the angel, "How shall I know this? For I am an old man, and my wife is well advanced in years." And the angel answered and said to him, "I am

Gabriel, who stands in the presence of God, and was sent to speak to you and bring you these glad tidings. **But behold, you will be mute and not able to speak until the day these things take place,** *because you did not believe my words* **which will be fulfilled in their own time"** (Luke 1:18-20).

But **when the fullness of the time had come,** *God sent forth His Son, born of a woman, born under the law* (Galatians 4:4).

So, no matter what you are going through now, just make sure you are in the place where God wants you and that you do what He commanded you to do. The rest is up to the Lord.

"Now My soul is troubled, and what shall I say? 'Father, save Me from this hour'? **But for this purpose I came to this hour** (John 12:27).

Chapter 14

GROWING OUR ROOTS

*What we don't see is what sustains
what our eyes admire.*

GROWING OUR ROOTS

*A*s we mentioned in the previous chapter, for you to reach the height to which the Lord will take you, it is of vital importance that your roots grow adequately to support you. And for this to happen, the Lord allows us to go through various processes, which include:

› *Starting with small tasks*
Everything that is great today was small at first. A promotion is a reward for good performance in a past level.

Our beginnings usually take place behind the scenes, and when we are ready, the Lord brings us out.

Jesse had seven of his sons pass before Samuel, but Samuel said to him, "The Lord has not chosen these." So he asked Jesse, "Are these all the sons you have?" "There is still the youngest," Jesse answered. "He is tending the sheep." Samuel said, "Send for him; we will not sit down until he arrives" (1 Samuel 16:10-11 NIV).

In other words, the prophet says to Jesse: "Bring him from his place because the Lord wants him here."

› Submit to the leadership of others

Although you might not like the authority that God has placed to guide you, because you don't approve of the person or consider the leader to be less educated than yourself, that person has been set by the Lord to lead you.

When you refuse to submit to a delegated authority, it is rebellion against God. Those that the Lord has placed in authority are His "direct representatives," and even if they don't proceed as you would expect them to, your role is to obey them and the Lord that placed them in authority will deal with them.

> *Our beginnings usually take place behind the scenes, and when we are ready, the Lord brings us out.*

Let everyone be subject to the governing authorities, **for there is no authority except that which God has established.** *The authorities that exist have been established by God. Consequently,* **whoever rebels against the authority is rebelling against what God has instituted,** *and those who do so will bring judgment on themselves* (Romans 13:1-2 NIV).

› Working for the ministry of others

Before you can become a teacher, you must first be a student. Before God puts people at your side to help you carry out the vision that He's given you, you must first work to help the fulfillment of a vision given to another.

In the Bible, we see how great leaders such as kings and conquerors were first good disciples, collaborators, and even served others.

> » Moses, the man God used to free His people from captivity, had first to feed the sheep of his father-in-law, Jethro.
> » The great conqueror, Joshua, was first the assistant of Moses, the one who lifted his hands when he got tired.
> » Before ascending to the throne, David, the great king of Israel, had to tend to his family's sheep and also do house chores.
> » Before Elisha was invested as a prophet, he was a faithful follower of Elijah.
> » Before Jesus began his ministry he submitted himself to be baptized by John, although John had said about Him:

*"There comes One after me who is **mightier than I,** whose sandal strap I am not worthy to stoop down and loose* (Mark 1:7).

In those times a disciple could do anything for his teacher, except untie the footwear, and this is because it was part of the duties of a slave; this was one of Jesus' most significant examples of submission, submitting to someone who in all respects was younger than Him.

*And John tried to prevent Him, saying, **"I need to be baptized by You, and are You coming to me?"** But Jesus answered and said to him, **"Permit it to be so now, for thus it is fitting** for us to fulfill all righteousness."*

131

Then he allowed Him (Matthew 3:14-15).

The Lord expects us to submit and give the best in our service to others. This is not a sign of inferiority, but the way God prepares a foundation for what He has prepared for us.

There's a story in which an old carpenter told the contractor, for whom he had worked many years, that he was planning to retire from the construction business to enjoy his family. He admitted that he would miss his work and his paycheck, but he understood that it was time to say goodbye. The contractor then asked the carpenter to build him one last house. To which the carpenter accepted. However, in doing so, he showed that his heart was no longer in the work that he did. He didn't put the same care in building and used materials of inferior quality.

When the carpenter finished the building, his employer came to inspect it and finally handed the house key to him saying: "This is now your house, it is my farewell gift." The carpenter was amazed and said: "What a pity. If I had known that I was building my own house, I would have done things so differently!"

Be careful how you build, because you could be making your own house.

Chapter 15

MIXTURES ARE UNACCEPTABLE

*Its internal structure does not allow mixtures
that are contrary to its essence.*

MIXTURES ARE UNACCEPTABLE

*I*n addition to having extensive and deep roots, the palm tree has another striking characteristic, it remains pure in the middle of the forest, without receiving the pollen that is transmitted from different sources, such as air, bees, and birds, between one tree and another. Its internal structure causes it to reject any mixture other than its very essence.

As an excellent example of this, we find in chapter 38 of the book of Genesis, which tells the story of Tamar, whose name means palm tree. She was the daughter-in-law of Judah, one of Jacob's sons.

Tamar's first husband was called Er, whom the Bible says he was wicked in the Lord's sight; so, the Lord put him to death (See Genesis 38:7).

When she became a widow, "Palm Tree" becomes the wife of Onan, Er's brother. According to Levirate law, a widowed woman, who didn't have children, was to marry one of the brothers of her deceased husband to continue the succession line and the family descent.

But in this regard here is what the Bible says:

*But Onan knew that the heir would not be his; and it came to pass, when he went in to his brother's wife, that he emitted on the ground, **lest he should give an heir to his brother. And the thing which he did displeased the Lord; therefore He killed him also.** Then Judah said to Tamar his daughter-in-law, "Remain a widow in your father's house till my son Shelah is grown." For he said, "Lest he also die like his brothers." And Tamar went and dwelt in her father's house* (Genesis 38:9-11).

According to the culture of that time, it was a shame for a woman, after being married, to return to her parents' home without a husband and with no children. But Tamar, out of obedience, faced the shame.

Time passed, and Shela became a man and Judah had not fulfilled his promise to her. Due to the widow's dark past, he didn't want to give this woman to her son thinking that Shela could suffer the same fate as his brothers. *For he said, "Lest he also die like his brothers"* (Genesis 38:11).

That's how Tamar became a forgotten woman, having to face shame, loneliness, and criticism for a long time from those who surrounded her.

And it is precisely by observing this story that we come to admire the attitude of this woman who brought honor to her name, by deciding not to mix with anyone outside the tribe of Judah, because she was only to procreate from that tribe. She could've quickly given up on this because if any party, (the widow or the man who had the responsibility to be her new husband) avoided moving forward with marriage, the other side had the opportunity to give up this right through a ceremony known as *"halizah."*

But even having this option, this "Palm Tree" decided to take a bold stance, to not mix with the inappropriate person.

*She pretended to be a harlot, and slept with her father-in-law, Judah (who was already a widower at that time) and got pregnant. Upon learning that his ex-daughter-in-law was pregnant, Judah was outraged, but realizing that he was the father, said: **"She has been more righteous than I, because I did not give her to Shelah my son." And he never knew her again*** (Genesis 38:26).

After such a sad episode in Tamar's life, God proceeds to give her the reward.

*Now it came to pass, at the time for giving birth, that behold, **twins were in her womb*** (Genesis 38:27).

And although she was forgotten by man for an extended period of her life, she was recognized by the Lord, as being one of the only four women who is later recorded in the Bible, in the genealogy of Jesus Christ (See Matthew 1:3). Something that she would have never reached if she had decided to mix with someone that was not from the house of Judah.

Just like the palm trees that preserve their purity, not allowing mixture, nor grafts, so the Lord calls us to live our lives in Him.

Chapter 16

ALWAYS BEARING FRUIT

*Its productivity does not cease
through the seasons.*

ALWAYS BEARING FRUIT

*U*nlike other plants, the palm tree does not bear fruit seasonally it produces year-round, its productivity does not stop.

The famous 17th-century botanist Carolus Linnaeus called the palm trees "the princesses of the plant kingdom." The reason for this is the way it grows, its long life, its continuous greenness, and to the fact that at the age of 50 it enters a process of change and transformation in its bark, which from that point onward begins to bear its best fruits.

As an example of this, we find that when Caleb appeared before Joshua, he said:

"...I was forty years old when Moses the servant of the Lord sent me from Kadesh Barnea to spy out the land, and I brought back word to him as it was in my heart. Nevertheless my brethren who went up with me made the heart of the people melt, but I wholly followed the Lord my God. So Moses swore on that day, saying, 'Surely the land where your foot has trodden shall be your inheritance and your children's forever, because

you have wholly followed the Lord my God.'

And now, behold, the Lord has kept me alive, as He said, these forty-five years, ever since the Lord spoke this word to Moses while Israel wandered in the wilderness; **and now, here I am this day, eighty-five years old. As yet I am as strong this day as on the day that Moses sent me; just as my strength was then, so now is my strength for war, both for going out and for coming in.** *Now therefore, give me this mountain of which the Lord spoke in that day; for you heard in that day how the Anakim were there, and that the cities were great and fortified. It may be that the Lord will be with me, and I shall be able to drive them out as the Lord said"* (Joshua 14:6-12).

As this passage reveals, Caleb's strengths were the same as on the day that Moses spoke with him. Even though forty-five years had passed, he was still as strong as back then.

Here we can appreciate the expression of the psalmist saying: *"The righteous shall flourish like a palm tree"* bearing fruit year-round and all the years of his life. Glory to God!

Give me this mountain

The fact that at the age of eighty-five Caleb says: "Give me this mountain" reveals his assurance in the God who had made the promise to him, since this place was inhabited by the Anakim (a tribe of giants descendants of Anak) and their cities were large and walled.

When considering the implications of such a difficult conquest, it is relevant to consider that Caleb, being a war veteran, could have been given another territory with fewer complications, such as the plains of Canaan, where the most fruitful valleys have the best streams of water. However, He said: "Give me this mountain." And although it was the most difficult of all places, it was his mountain, according to the promise that had received 45 years before.

And even though he knew the difficult part of the territory, far from being intimidated he said: *"Only do not rebel against the Lord, nor fear the people of the land, for **they are our bread;** their protection has departed from them, and the Lord is with us. Do not fear them"* (Numbers 14:9).

With his example Caleb shows us that age is no matter, we can look to the mountain that has been promised to us and say to the sons of Anak: "Get out of my mountain!"

Remember that palm trees don't stop their productivity in any season of the year. Therefore, regain strength and undertake to conquer whatever your mountain is.

Chapter 17

USEFULNESS OF FRUIT

Bears fruit all year-round
and none its fruit is useless.

USEFULNESS OF FRUIT

*R*egarding productivity, the palm tree can have up to 360 different uses. It is not only its fruit but also its trunk, leaves, and roots that are useful to man.

The fruit of the palm tree has healing properties for diseases of the respiratory system and intestinal tract. It is used for detoxification, purification, and cleansing of organs. With its branches, a wide variety of things are made such as roofs, walls, palisades, baskets and many kinds of ornaments.

In each season of the year, we find certain crops that only occur in a particular season. For example:

In spring: avocado, pear, and cherry are harvested; in the Summer: melon, watermelon, strawberry, among others; during the fall season: lemon, tangerine, apple and others, and in winter mostly citrus fruits are produced like kiwi, orange, and others.

But as we observed in the previous chapter, unlike all these fruit trees, the palm tree produces its fruit year-round, and **none of its fruit is useless.** As the palm tree, which produces year-round its useful fruit, the Lord expects us to bear continuous results and be able to heal and detoxify the environment where we have been planted.

The Christian preacher and writer, John Bunyan, once said: *"If my life is fruitless, it does not matter who praises me, and if my life is fruitful, it does not matter who criticizes me."*

When people approached George Fox, founder of the Quaker Christian movement, stating that they were saved because they had believed in Jesus, Fox's question to them was: "What is the fruit of your belief?"

Jesus said, *"For a good tree does not bear bad fruit, nor does a bad tree bear good fruit. For every tree is known by its own fruit* (Luke 6:43).

Based on this passage we can see that "the fruit" is made up of attitudes, and actions that define the life of a person.

In the book of Galatians, Paul references the fruit produced by the Spirit in the lives of those who have accepted His government.

But the *fruit of the Spirit is love, joy, peace, forbearance, kindness, goodness, faithfulness, gentleness and self-control* (Galatians 5:22, 23a NIV).

Let's see the meaning of this fruit in each of its parts, according to the Greek:

Love *(agape)***:** Affection, benevolence, love.

It denotes affection, goodwill, benevolence and an affectionate spirit. Having this fruit implies having the ability, the power, and the determination to love the people we don't desire. It also means to seek another person's well-being without conditions or waiting for anything in return.

Joy *(jara)*: Joy, delight, calmness.

It alludes to rejoicing, being happy and full of joy, regardless of the circumstances. The term does not imply being happy because happiness is a state of mind, based on the circumstances of the moment. Joy produces its fruit continually because it is based on being content with God's care and kindness, no matter what the conditions are.

Peace *(eirene)*: Prosperity, peace.

It refers to the tranquility or serenity of spirit. This fruit represents a blessing based on the relationship with God, which allows the possessor to live with others in harmony and tranquility.

Forbearance *(makrodsumia)*: Long-suffering, support, endurance.

It implies bearing something without getting upset; denoting balance between temperament and passions. When there is patience there is consistency, firmness, and perseverance; the person who is patient is tolerant and lenient. The term also implies resistance, showing a high level of tolerance.

Kindness *(jestotes)*: Utility, excellence, character, patience, goodness.

It refers to the softness of character, tranquility of the spirit. To have a relaxed disposition to treat others with courtesy.

Goodness *(agadsosume)*: Virtue or beneficence.

The term applies to the righteousness of the heart, which manifests in our life showing sincerity, integrity, honesty, and always choosing to do the right thing, even if at a cost.

Faithfulness (*pistis*): Persuasion, credibility, truthfulness, conviction, trust, perseverance, fidelity.

It consists in believing in something even when common sense says something different; it is to put our trust in God's vision and not what we see.

Gentleness (*praotes*): Gentleness, humility.

It describes the humility of a person to be guided by others, showing respect and courtesy.

Self-Control (*enkrateia*): Self-control, self-restraint.

It refers to exercising control over lust, the ability to restrain instincts, appetites, and impulses, to serve the Lord with sobriety and discipline.

PART THREE

GROWING AT EVERY LEVEL

Chapter 18

HOW TO STEP UP TO THE NEXT LEVEL?

That the man of God may be complete,
thoroughly equipped for every good work
(2 Timothy 3:17).

HOW TO STEP UP TO THE NEXT LEVEL?

*S*o far, we have focused on the need to grow, on two main foundations:

1. The parable of the fig tree, alluding to our need to be fruitful to fulfill God's expectations of us (Luke 13:6-9).

2. The palm tree, considering its four primordial characteristics (the depth of its roots, which it does not mix, its continuous productivity and the usefulness of its fruit) we should consider that we have been called to flourish in the same way (Psalm 92:12).

However, as we reach the last part of this book, we will consider other important points about our growth.

God's Word teaches us that our Lord Jesus Christ **grew in wisdom, stature, and grace before God and men** and He set an example for us to imitate, **let's follow His example** (See John 13:15).

Before continuing, it is important to remember that the Bible says:

*All Scripture is God-breathed and is **useful for teaching,*** *rebuking, correcting **and training in righteousness, so that the servant of God may be thoroughly equipped for every good work** (2 Timothy 3:16-17).*

The word of God has no waste. Everything written in Scripture has a fundamental purpose in our lives, including the stories and the experiences that our fellow servants-in-the-Lord have had.

Based on this, I invite you to consider the following story, which I hope you won't only read but also carefully analyze, since it contains key teachings, that when put into practice will supernaturally bless your life.

And it came to pass, when the Lord was about to take up Elijah into heaven by a whirlwind, that Elijah went with Elisha from Gilgal. Then Elijah said to Elisha, "Stay here, please, for the Lord has sent me on to Bethel." But Elisha said, "As the Lord lives, and as your soul lives, I will not leave you!" So they went down to Bethel.

Now the sons of the prophets who were at Bethel came out to Elisha, and said to him, "Do you know that the Lord will take away your master from over you today?" And he said, "Yes, I know; keep silent!" Then Elijah said to him, "Elisha, stay here, please, for the Lord has sent me on to Jericho." But he said, "As the Lord lives, and as your soul lives, I will not leave you!" So they came to Jericho. Now the sons of the prophets who were at Jericho came to Elisha and said to him, "Do you know that the Lord will take away your master from over you today?" So he answered, "Yes, I know; keep silent!" Then Elijah said to him, "Stay here, please, for the Lord has sent me on to the Jordan." But he said, "As the Lord lives, and as your soul lives, I will not leave you!" So the two of them went on. And fifty men of the sons of the prophets went and stood facing them at a distance, while the two of them stood by the Jordan. Now Elijah took his mantle, rolled it up, and struck the water; and it was divided this way and that, so that the two of them crossed over on dry ground. And so it was, when they had crossed over, that Elijah said to Elisha, "Ask! What may I do for you, before I am taken away from you?" Elisha said, "Please let a double portion of your spirit be upon me." So he said, "You have asked a hard thing. Nevertheless, if you see me when I am taken from you, it shall be so for you; but if not, it shall not be so." Then it happened, as they continued on and talked, that suddenly a chariot of fire appeared with horses of fire, and separated the two of them; and Elijah went up by a whirlwind into heaven. And Elisha saw it, and he cried out, "My father, my father, the chariot of Israel and its horsemen!" So he saw him no more. And he took hold of his own clothes and tore them into two pieces (2 Kings 2:1-12).

If all the things that were written in the past were written to teach us, what can we learn from Scripture, that will take us to the next level? Let's look at this by part.

First level: Circumcision

This story emphasizes the names of the places that were visited, the first one is Gilgal.

Gilgal is literally translated as: "circle of stones." This place was Israel's first encampment after crossing the Jordan River. Furthermore, it was the starting point for the military campaigns led by Joshua (See Joshua 4:19-24; 5:10; 10:6-7, 15).

But the most sobering event that happened there

was that God commanded Joshua to **circumcise the Israelites.**

At that time the Lord said to Joshua, "Make flint knives for yourself, and circumcise the sons of Israel again the second time." **So Joshua made flint knives for himself, and circumcised the sons of Israel at the hill of the foreskins.**

So it was, when they had finished circumcising all the people, that they stayed in their places in the camp till they were healed. Then the Lord said to Joshua, "This day I have rolled away the reproach of Egypt from you." Therefore the name of the place is called Gilgal to this day (Joshua 5:2-5, 8-9).

> *The real circumcision is that of the heart, which happens when we rid ourselves of all envy, jealousy, gossip, strife, roots of bitterness, resentment, hatred, rejection, and everything that damages our heart.*

Taking this into perspective, as Elisha did, the first place where people must go before stepping up to the next level is "Gilgal." Gilgal is the place of *circumcision,* where the reproach of Egypt is rolled away, and the identity of a "true Israelite" is acquired, that of a true child of God.

You may be thinking to yourself: So, are you suggesting that all males of this time must be circumcised, even after Christ's sacrifice? The answer is: Not in the way that Joshua did it, but as the apostle

Paul explains it in the book of Romans.

For he is not a Jew who is one outwardly, nor is circumcision that which is outward in the flesh; but he is a Jew who is one inwardly; and **circumcision is that of the heart, in the Spirit...** (Romans 2:28-29).

The real circumcision is that of the heart, which happens when we rid ourselves of all envy, jealousy, gossip, strife, roots of bitterness, resentment, hatred, rejection, and everything that damages our heart.

This only occurs when we are full of the fruit of the Spirit as we read in Galatians 5:22, and discussed in this book in the previous chapter.

Therefore, stepping up to the next level is going through the "spiritual Gilgal," the place where our hearts are circumcised, all ungodliness is rolled away, and we become filled with the fruit of the Holy Spirit.

Second level: Experience

According to our base Scripture, the second place where Elijah and Elisha passed was Bethel.

Bethel, in Hebrew, means "House of God," and it is the name of a Canaanite city of the old region of Samaria, located in the center of the land of Canaan. But who named it like that and why? Let's read the story:

Now Jacob went out from Beersheba and went toward Haran. So he came to a certain place and stayed there all night, because the sun had set. And he took one of the stones of that place and put it at his head, and he lay down in that place to sleep. Then he dreamed, and behold, a ladder was set up on the earth, and its top reached to heaven; and there the angels of God were ascending and descending on it.

And behold, the Lord stood above it and said: "I am the Lord God of Abraham your father and the God of Isaac; the land on which you lie I will give to you and your descendants. Also your descendants shall be as the dust of the earth; you shall spread abroad to the west and the east, to the north and the south; and in you and in your seed all the families of the earth shall be blessed. Behold, **I am with you and will keep you wherever you go, and will bring you back to this land; for I will not leave you until I have done what I have spoken to you."** *Then Jacob awoke from his sleep and said, "Surely the Lord is in this place, and I did not know it." And he was afraid and said, "How awesome is this place! This is none other than the house of God, and this is the gate of heaven!" Then Jacob rose early in the morning, and took the stone that he had put at his head, set it up as a pillar, and poured oil on top of it. And he called the name of that place Bethel; but the name of that city had been Luz previously* (Genesis 28:10-19).

So, Jacob named the place after having the most awesome experience of his life, where God established a covenant promising to bless him, to give him the land, and not leave him until He fulfills all the promises given to Jacob. Therefore, *Bethel is the place of experience.*

The second place where you must pass through on your journey to your next level up is Bethel. Because that's where you'll have the "experience" that will change your life.

After his Bethel experience, years later, we see that Esau goes out to find his brother Jacob to kill him for having taken his birthright, in an "illegitimate" way, something we know had already been determined by the Lord, because He declared it to Rebekah when t two brothers were still being conceived in her womb.

"Two nations are in your womb, two peoples shall be separated from your body; **One people shall be stronger than the other, And the older shall serve the younger"** (Genesis 25:23).

But the moment of revenge had come. Esau was ready to kill Jacob and had an army of four hundred armed men with him, who were waiting for the order to begin the massacre. But the question is, why does Jacob decide to see his brother, knowing that he was putting his life in danger? (See Genesis 33).

The answer is that Jacob said within himself: "My brother can't kill me because God appeared to me in a personal experience and gave me the land which I was laying on, and He promised to bless and protect me until everything he spoke is fulfilled."

> *When you have your own experience with the Lord, you will know where you are going, and the One Who is taking you. Consequently, false statements won't affect you; words of discouragement won't depress you, and no one can destroy you even if they want to.*

Jacob's intimate and personal experience prepared him to face fearlessly any situation until the fulfillment of all of God's promises to him. When you have your own experience with the Lord, you will know where you are going, and the One who is taking you. Consequently, false statements won't affect you; words of discouragement won't depress you, and no one can destroy you even if they want to.

On the other hand, when Peter was severely threatened by the authorities, imprisoned, and whipped, he armed himself of courage and said: *For we can't but speak the things which we have seen and heard."* In other words, he was saying: "Gentlemen this isn't something someone else told me about, I personally experienced it in my own flesh. I saw the Lord Jesus doing miracles; I saw Him walking on the waters, I was with Him while He brought the dead to life and so many other things. So, if you want to kill me go ahead, but I will never stop speaking of the things that I have seen and heard."

The Lord is interested in everyone having their own experience with Him because only then, our roots will be deep-seated, and our foundation will be solid.

Third Level: Obedience

The third place where the characters of this passage go through is Jericho.

Jericho is derived from the Hebrew word *(iareaj)* which means "moon." One of the most remarkable events occurred there, let's read:

Now Jericho was securely shut up because of the children of Israel; none went out, and none came in. And the Lord said to Joshua: "See! I have given Jericho into your hand, its king, and the mighty men of valor. You shall march around the city, all you men of war; you shall go all around the city once. This you shall do six days. And seven priests shall bear seven trumpets of rams' horns before the ark. But the seventh day you shall march around the city seven times, and the priests shall blow the trumpets. **It shall come to pass, when they make a long blast with the ram's horn, and when you hear the sound of the trumpet, that all the people shall shout with a great shout; then the wall of the city will fall down flat.** *And the people shall go up every man straight before him"* (Joshua 6:1-5).

These are the instructions that God gave to Joshua:

> » All the mighty men of valor are to surround the city.
> » Go around the city once for six days.
> » Seven priests shall carry seven trumpets of ram's horns in front of the ark.
> » On the seventh day, march seven times around the city.
> » On the seventh day, the priests shall blow the trumpets.
> » The priests shall make a long blast with the ram's horn.
> » All the people are to shout with a great shout.

After the Lord had given these instructions to Joshua, He declares that *the wall of the city will fall down flat.*

But, what is the essence that we want to extract from what happened here?

That in addition to this, there is no historical record anywhere in the world, indicating that the walls of a city so big and so great, collapsed because a group of people walked around it, singing and playing trumpets. Which means that this required a very high level of obedience on Joshua's part to fulfill the mandate of God.

In this context, Jericho is the spiritual place where one must obey God's command, even if what is commanded does not make sense to you.

It's only when we operate at the *Jericho* spiritual level that we can fulfill the Lord's commands, like the one given to us in Matthew 5:38-44:

Bless those that curse you, **do good** to those that do evil to you, love your enemies, **pray** for those that persecute you, whoever forces you to go one mile, **go with them two miles.**

> *Jericho is the spiritual place where one must obey God's command, even if what is commanded does not make sense to you.*

To be able to forgive, love, obey and be faithful to God in everything He commands us to do, we must go through "Jericho," because at this place human reasoning does not dominate our mind, and emotions don't rule over us. Reaching this level can be a significant challenge for many people. However, those that succeed at getting there, have high heavenly privileges, for the Lord clearly said:

*If you abide in Me, and **My words abide in you, you will ask what you desire, and it shall be done for you*** (John 15:7).

Fourth level: Endued with the supernatural

Returning to Scripture, we see that after going to Jericho, Elijah and Elisha go to the Jordan.

Jordan means "the one that descends," because it flows to a lower elevation. At its birthplace, it is 520 meters above sea level, and it travels downstream to an elevation of 392 meters, flowing into the Dead Sea. It also means: "the perennial river" that lasts forever.

Among the incredible events that occurred at this river, the Scripture records that after Elijah and Elisha passed through the places that we mentioned before they went to the Jordan, and before crossing it, the prophet Elijah takes off his mantle, struck the waters, and the waters divided into two parts. Let's read what the Scripture says:

Then Elijah said to him, "Stay here, please, for the Lord has sent me on to the Jordan." But he said, "As the Lord lives, and as your soul lives, I will not leave you!" So the two of them went on. And fifty men of the sons of the prophets went and stood facing them at a distance, while the two of them stood by the Jordan. Now Elijah took his mantle, rolled it up, and struck the water; and it was divided this way and that, so that the two of them crossed over on dry ground. And so it was, when they had crossed over, that Elijah said to Elisha, "Ask! What may I do for you, before I am taken away from you?" Elisha said, "Please let a double portion of your spirit be upon me."

So he said, "You have asked a hard thing. *Nevertheless, if you see me when I am taken from you, it shall be so for you; but if not, it shall not be so." Then it happened, as they continued on and talked, that suddenly a chariot of fire appeared with horses of fire, and separated the two of them; and Elijah went up by a whirlwind into heaven. And Elisha saw it, and he cried out, "My father, my father, the chariot of Israel and its horsemen!" So he* *saw him no more. And he took hold of his own clothes and tore them into two pieces* (2 Kings 2:6-12).

Observe that when the time comes for the farewell, Elijah says to Elisha: "Ask! What may I do for you, before I am taken away from you?"

It's intriguing that when Elisha asks for the double portion of his spirit, Elijah replies: **"You have asked a hard thing."**

The word "hard," refers to something that is not easily achieved, in other words, it is unlikely to happen, it is not something easy to comprehend, it requires a unique set of skills, effort and lots of work.

So, why does Elijah say that Elisha's request is hard when the only requirement to receive the double portion was to see him at the moment he is taken away? Common sense would dictate that seeing someone go is not hard. The only thing that we need to see is sight.

However, this is precisely the problem: the flesh (natural) cannot see the spiritual things (See 1 Corinthians 2:14).

Therefore, what Elijah is implying to Elisha is: "What you are asking for does not depend on me, it will depend on how you can see things in the spiritual realm. Because what's going to happen, when I am taken away, is totally spiritual."

Now this I say, brethren, that flesh and blood cannot inherit the kingdom of God; nor does corruption inherit incorruption (1 Corinthians 15:50).

So, when Elijah was transformed, everything would be part of the spiritual world, not visible to the natural eye. This is what the prophet was referring to when he said: *"If you see me when I am taken from you, it shall be so for you; but if not, it shall not be so."*

Chapter 19

YOU MUST SEE IT

...And Elijah saw it.

YOU MUST SEE IT

*T*hen it happened, as they continued on and talked, that suddenly a chariot of fire appeared with horses of fire, and separated the two of them; and Elijah went up by a whirlwind into heaven. **And Elisha saw it,** and he cried out, "My father, my father, the chariot of Israel and its horsemen!" So he saw him no more. And he took hold of his own clothes and tore them into two pieces (2 Kings 2:11-12).

How did Elisha see it?

Elisha's spiritual sight was so in tune with the spirit realm that not only did he see Elijah go up in the whirlwind, but also the spiritual chariots and horses. Therefore, we can say that Elisha was highly qualified to receive what he had asked for.

As for the prophets, according to Scripture, they stood facing them at a distance; unlike Elisha, who saw the whole event occur, they did not. As we read on, the prophets thought that Elijah had gone somewhere else, and sent a search party out for three days but did not find him.

Then they said to him, "Look now, there are fifty strong men with your servants. **Please let them go and search for your master, lest perhaps the Spirit of the Lord has taken him up and cast him upon some mountain or into some valley."** *And he said, "You shall not send anyone." But when they urged him till he was ashamed, he said, "Send them!" Therefore they sent fifty men, and they searched for three days but did not find him. And when they came back to him, for he had stayed in Jericho, he said to them, "Did I not say to you, 'Do not go'?"* (2 Kings 2:16-18).

The Jordan is a place where the supernatural descends. But the only ones that can enter at this level are those that can operate in it.

Operating in the supernatural

After going through Gilgal (the place of the circumcision), Bethel (the place of experience), Jericho (the place of obedience) and Jordan where we are invested with the power from on high is that we will be ready to operate in the supernatural.

After Elisha received his request, he continued to see things that others could not, because the spiritual world was open to him.

On one occasion, the prophet visualized the ambush that the Syrians planned against the people of Israel while nobody else saw it.

Now the king of Syria was making war against Israel; and he consulted with his servants, saying, "My camp will be in such and such a place." **And the man of God sent to the king of Israel, saying, "Beware that you do not pass this place, for the Syrians are coming down there."** *Then the king of Israel sent someone to the place of which the* *man of God had told him. Thus he warned him, and he was watchful there, not just once or twice. Therefore the heart of the king of Syria was greatly troubled by this thing; and he called his servants and said to them, "Will you not show me which of us is for the king of Israel?" And one of his servants said, "None, my lord, O king; **but Elisha, the prophet who is in Israel, tells the king of Israel the words that you speak in your bedroom"*** (2 Kings 6:8-12).

Elisha could also clearly see the thousands of enemies that went to attack him in the vision he had in his room in Dothan, while his servant could not see it. However, Elisha prayed to God, and the servant's eyes were also opened, and he was able to see what Elisha was seeing.

So he said, *"Go and see where he is, that I may send and get him." And it was told him, saying, "Surely he is in Dothan." Therefore he sent horses and chariots and a great army there, and they came by night and surrounded the city. And when the servant of the man of God arose early and went out, there was an army, surrounding the city with horses and chariots. **And his servant said to him, "Alas, my master! What shall we do?" So he answered, "Do not fear, for those who are with us are more than those who are with them." And Elisha prayed, and said, "Lord, I pray, open his eyes that he may see." Then the Lord opened the eyes of the young man, and he saw. And behold, the mountain was full of horses and chariots of fire all around Elisha*** (2 Kings 6:13-17).

On another occasion, while sitting in his house with the elders of Israel, Elisha was able to see beforehand how some murderers came to try to apprehend and capture him; while the others only saw them when they arrived.

But Elisha was sitting in his house, and the elders were sitting with him. And the king sent a man ahead of him, **but before the messenger came to him, he said to the elders, "Do you see how this son of a murderer has sent someone to take away my head?** *Look, when the messenger comes, shut the door, and hold him fast at the door. Is not the sound of his master's feet behind him?"* (2 Kings 6:32).

Since this level can't be understood in the natural realm, only in the spiritual realm, this level will usually confuse those who don't operate in it. Let's see this example:

Now the Angel of the Lord came and sat under the terebinth tree which was in Ophrah, which belonged to Joash the Abiezrite, while his son **Gideon threshed wheat in the winepress, in order to hide it from the Midianites. And the Angel of the Lord appeared to him, and said to him, "The Lord is with you, you mighty man of valor!"** (Judges 6:11-12).

A person who views things only in the natural realm, when considering the words said by the angel, could ask, how can Gideon be called a brave and courageous man when he was terrified, shaking the wheat to hide it from the Midianites? But the angel, as a representative sent from Heaven, didn't just see Gideon shaking the wheat to hide it, but the man that would later be used by the Lord to deliver His people from the Midianites.

Something similar happened at Paul's calling. Ananias was asked to go and pray for Saul so that he could recover his sight; he didn't fully understand what God was asking him to do because his natural perception only saw a Saul who was a cruel persecutor of the church and had aided in the deaths of many believers. But from Heaven's perspective, Paul was seen as the writer of Colossians, Corinthians, Galatians and all the influential books that Paul later wrote.

This same level of revelation came to the blind man in Bethsaida healed by Jesus, to which the Lord asked him if he saw anything. And the man said, **"I see men like trees, walking."**

Anyone who reads this story can think that anyone seeing men as trees indicates that the miracle went wrong. However, to really understand what happened we must recall what was said by the psalmist about man.

He shall be like **a tree planted by the rivers of water,** *that brings forth its fruit in its season, whose leaf also shall not wither; and whatever he does shall prosper* (Psalm 1:3).

Observe that the psalmist's expression is: "shall be like a tree planted by the rivers of water"; which is saying that there is a dimension in the lives of human beings that compares to trees planted by the rivers of water. Therefore, the blind man receives not only his natural sight but also a vision to see beyond what at first glance can be seen. The blind man was able to see that those who walked with the Lord (His disciples) were common men at simple sight, but in the spiritual sense they are like *a tree planted by the rivers of water,* which represents Jesus.

Chapter 20

SIDE EFFECTS OF SPIRITUAL GROWTH

Higher levels of growth,
higher levels of attack.

SIDE EFFECTS OF SPIRITUAL GROWTH

*I*t is impossible that your promotion to new levels will come alone. As long as your growth is a threat to the kingdom of darkness, the side effects of your spiritual growth will become visible. Sometimes the evidence of being effective at what God has called you to do is manifested in the intense battles you must continually wage.

The sign that we have reached new levels of growth is the increase in pressure to which we are exposed.

Some time ago, I was going through a challenging situation, and when I turned to the Lord in prayer to ask Him what was the reason for the attack I was facing, He led me to read Luke 4:1-2, which says:

Then Jesus, being filled with the Holy Spirit, returned from the Jordan and was led by the Spirit into the wilderness, being tempted for forty days by the devil. And in those days He ate nothing, and afterward, when they had ended, He was hungry.

Although I had read this passage many times over, I felt that day that the Lord was using it to minister to me in a special way.

And unlike other times, my attention was drawn to the fact that Satan came personally to tempt to Jesus while He was in the wilderness.

After seeing this, it helped me to understand that before Satan attacks someone, he takes his time to do a detailed and profound analysis of weaknesses, virtues, vulnerable areas, and the open doors that the person has left in the spiritual world. Then he plans his attack according to the vulnerabilities the individual may have in his spiritual life.

When Jesus of Nazareth went into the wilderness, the enemy made his own analysis and realizes that the person who he is going to deal with is nothing less than the King of kings and Lord of lords, the Alpha and the Omega, the Highest Expression of Power. So, when Satan starts analyzing who he was going to send to tempt him, he suddenly realized that he was facing the only One worthy of opening the seals in Heaven, and then, clearly, for the war to make sense the greatest of the abysses had to go personally.

Therefore, what God wanted to help me understand is that when the levels of revelation, glory, and integrity, grow in us, the attack levels are also increased against us; this is because we become a higher threat to the devices and plans of darkness, than ever before.

War of concepts

I want to clarify that when we are operating in the supernatural dimension certain levels of spiritual warfare increase, more than a war between God and the devil, it's rather a war of concepts. For example, let's look at the following passages:

I know that the Lord is great, that our Lord is greater than all gods. **The Lord does whatever pleases him, in the heavens and on the earth, in the seas and all their depths.** *He makes clouds rise from the ends of the earth; he sends lightning with the rain and brings out the wind from his storehouses* (Psalm 135:5-7 NIV).

> *The sign that we have reached new levels of growth is the increase in pressure to which we are exposed.*

The seventy-two returned with joy and said, "Lord, even the demons submit to us in your name." He replied, **"I saw Satan fall like lightning from heaven. I have given you authority to trample on snakes and scorpions and to overcome all the power of the enemy; nothing will harm you** (Luke 10:17-19 NIV).

The Lord said to Satan, "Where have you come from?" Satan answered the Lord, "From roaming throughout the earth, going back and forth on it." *Then the Lord said to Satan, "Have you considered my servant Job? There is no one on earth like him; he is blameless and upright, a man who fears God and shuns evil." "Does Job fear God for nothing?" Satan replied. "Have you not put a hedge around him and his household and everything he has? You have blessed the work of his hands, so that his flocks and herds are spread throughout the land. But now stretch out your hand and strike everything he has, and he will surely curse you to your face."* **The Lord said to**

Satan, "Very well, then, everything he has is in your power, but on the man himself do not lay a finger." Then Satan went out from the presence of the Lord (Job 1:7-12 NIV).

Then I looked and heard the voice of many angels, numbering thousands upon thousands, and ten thousand times ten thousand. They encircled the throne and the living creatures and the elders. In a loud voice they were saying: "Worthy is the Lamb, who was slain, to receive power and wealth and wisdom and strength and honor and glory and praise!" **Then I heard every creature in heaven and on earth and under the earth and on the sea, and all that is in them, saying: "To him who sits on the throne and to the Lamb be praise and honor and glory and power, for ever and ever!"** (Revelation 5:11-13 NIV).

Now I want us to consider this analysis carefully:

1. If Psalm 135 declares, that our Lord is **greater than all gods** and that the Lord does whatever pleases him, in the heavens and on the earth, in the seas and all their depths...

2. If the book of Job, reveals that Satan wanted to harm one of God's children, but **he first needed authorization from the Lord to do that...**

3. If the passage from Luke, tells us that **we were given the power to trample on snakes and scorpions and to overcome all the power of the enemy; and that nothing would hurt us...**

If this is so, why does Satan manage to destroy homes, families, churches, and ministries?

How can he go into those places if the angel of Lord encamps around those who fear Him and defends them?

To put it in a clear perspective, let's look at this example:

Think for a moment that you are in a house, where there are more than a thousand police officers, five helicopters surveying above the house, fifty war tanks surrounding the house, twenty-five snipers and forty security cameras watching the whole house. And suddenly two thieves enter the house, steal everything and leave on foot. You might say: But how can they do that?

How can two thieves go into a house full of police officers, on the ground and in the air, security cameras, snipers, and other security elements to protect the place? How do you suppose they got in? The answer is simple; they entered through the door. They robbed the place and left by the same door they came in, without anyone to stop them.

Let me tell you about something that happened at a very influential church that I know, where a terrible division occurred. In the beginning I didn't understand the reason for this, so I asked the Lord: Why did that church go through a split? How was Satan able to get inside a house that was filled with the power of God, miracles, healing, and signs and wonders?

Then, I understood that a door had been opened to him. Since there were several leaders in the congregation that had strife among themselves. Then the Lord took me to Matthew 12:24-26, where Jesus says that **a kingdom divided against itself will not stand.** So, what happened is that when the demon of division entered to destroy the church, some angels probably stopped it at the door.

But when they stopped him, the demon presented an arrest warrant, which consisted of Matthew 12:24-26 where Jesus said that a "kingdom," (a house, a church, a community, a business) divided against itself, it will not prosper.

So, the only thing they had to show the guardian angels at the door, were the Bible verses of this passage and then say: "Everything that Jesus says must be executed in heaven and on earth and underneath the earth. So, if in the church there are leaders who don't talk to each other, it means that the congregation can't and should not prosper."

The same thing happened in the days of Joshua with a bar of gold and a Babylonian mantle that Achan took illegally. Joshua says to the Lord: But what did I do? How could such a simple enemy defeat me? Am I not your child? And the answer is revealed as follows:

"Yes, you are my child, but there is an open door left by one of those that belong to your work team."

*But Israel **violated the instructions about the things set apart** for the Lord. A man named Achan had stolen some of these dedicated things, **so the Lord was very angry with the Israelites*** (Joshua 7:1 NLT).

In the economic aspect, the same scenario occurs. People stop tithing and offering and then attempt to rebuke the devourer. The Bible clearly states that the Lord is the one who rebukes for us the devourer for us when we are faithful with our finances (See Malachi 3:7-11).

Finally, it is dangerous to reach high spiritual positions without knowing the correct levels of warfare.

Any mishandle could end up in a massacre. Let's read the following example:

The bad advice of some of the princes of Ammon to king Hanun, after David sent word to comfort him for the death of his father, ended with the annihilation of thousands of people. Forty-thousand foot soldiers died because the king occupying the high position of the land didn't have a vision or the adequate level of understanding to operate in that position (See 2 Samuel 10:1-8).

Can you imagine, the churches that have been divided because one of the "princes of Ammon" (someone without vision) gave terrible advice to a leader that hasn't yet reached an understanding of the supernatural?

Do you have any idea of the number of good friendships and divine connections, which have been divided, only by the poisoned opinions of the "Ammonites"?

Don't be one of them, develop your vision and fight with the adequate weapons. Don't let your growth, or that of your house or your church become stagnant for no reason!

FINAL WORDS

*I*n closing, I want to remind you that the fact that you have been born is the evidence that there is something you must do, a mission for which you are designed to fulfill and no one else can replaced you. Only you can reveal and contribute to the world the specific deposits which you were born with.

Therefore, I encourage you to understand that you were created by God with a purpose, He has invested in you and expects you to maximize everything He has given to you. His delight is to see you grow, so please Him.

Reach that for which you were created; obey Him in everything and keep his commandments so that it goes well with you and you become successful and prosperous.

For then you will make your way prosperous, and then you will have good success. Have I not commanded you? **Be strong and of good courage; do not be afraid, nor be dismayed,** *for the Lord your God is with you wherever you go"* (Joshua 1:8b-9).

Made in the USA
Las Vegas, NV
12 June 2021